Apocalypse Child

01 02 03 04 05 28 27 26 25 24

Caitlin Press Inc.
3375 Ponderosa Way
Qualicum Beach, BC V9K 2J8
www.caitlinpress.com

Text design by Vici Johnstone
Cover design by Sarah Corsie
Cover photo by Martin Vysoudil (Unsplash)
Edited by Ruth Daniell
Printed in Canada

Caitlin Press Inc. acknowledges financial support from the Government of Canada and the Canada Council for the Arts, and the Province of British Columbia through the British Columbia Arts Council and the Book Publisher's Tax Credit.

Library and Archives Canada Cataloguing in Publication

Apocalypse child / Carly Butler.
Butler, Carly, author.
Canadiana 20230522467 | ISBN 9781773861326 (softcover)
LCSH: Butler, Carly. | LCSH: Judgment Day. | LCSH: Year 2000 date conversion (Computer
systems) | LCSH: Evangelicalism. | LCSH: Survivalism—Canada. | LCSH: Christian biography—Canada.
| LCGFT: Autobiographies.
LCC BT883 .B88 2024 | DDC 236/.9—dc23

Apocalypse Child

Surviving Doomsday and the Search for Identity at the End of the World

Carly Butler

Caitlin Press 2024

For all the Pascua-Yaqui relatives whose stories got lost, and all the other church kids who grew to tell the truth.

This is a true story that explores mature themes of sexuality, racism, abuse, language, pregnancy loss, medical peril and death of a child, as well as overall religious trauma. Please read with care.

Contents

Part Two - 61

Part Three - 139

Part Four - 173

Prologue

I stopped looking for the Apocalypse long ago, but every once in a while, I wondered if it still looked for me. My childhood days, weeks, months bled into each other as the years went by, but some of the smells and sounds and sights would never leave my memory.

Today, years later, a cold snap in the weather took me back to that cabin in an instant.

I could smell the winter chill before I felt it. Maybe it was because I'd burrowed myself so deeply inside my blanket, exposing only my nose for air, or maybe it was the stale, brittle quality of a log house that hadn't been warmed in hours. Either way, my eyes abruptly opened as I realized the fire must have gone out in the night. Now I'd have to start over. Would the firewood I'd chopped yesterday even be dry enough to use yet? I groaned and rolled over, not ready to move.

My ears ached; I had fallen asleep listening to music through my headphones again. I could still hear Michael W. Smith leading a worship song. The sound was watery and muffled, evidence that my Discman was suffering from a dying battery. I pulled the headphones off my ears in annoyance and shut the Discman off. *Stop being wasteful. What are you going to do when there are no more batteries?*

"Sing the songs myself," I muttered as I finally threw my blanket off and sat up. A shudder rippled through my adolescent body, making my bones ache with cold even though I was wearing an oversized t-shirt, flannel pajama pants and wool socks. Before my mom and I came here, I wore thin nightgowns to bed, but now I was used to adding layers. As I put the weight of my feet down I heard a loud crack through the floor. I reached down to the end of my bed for my sweater and toque. Mom was asleep in the cabin's original bedroom, on one side of our Jack-and-Jill bathroom, and I was on the other side, in the pantry that was just large enough for my bed and dresser. Thankfully, it also had a window, and I gently lifted the curtain to let the morning light in. Frost swirled the glass like lace. It must have been at least twenty below outside, which felt cruel, but at least it meant it likely wouldn't snow again today.

During our first winter here, Mom met a guy named Dave who had a tractor plough. The local logging company paid him to clear McDonell Lake Road past the ski hill, whenever needed. Our road, off Hankin Lake, branched away from McDonell for four kilometres before it reached our property and wasn't logged anymore, so Mom offered to pay Dave extra if he could come by our place whenever possible. He didn't always have time, but it felt like Christmas when he showed up. It meant I could leave this place at least one more time.

Don't think about that, I warned myself as I walked past the front door and into the kitchen. Too late, I ducked down beneath the front window as I heard a chorus of ungodly bleating begin outside. Mom had the animal pens built way too close to the cabin, and now every morning when they saw the slightest movement, the sheep and goats begged for hay as though it was their last meal. Eventually it would be, once we learned how to butcher and cure their meat. It was another task on our Apocalypse to-do list. I suspected Mom was procrastinating. Her belief in the Apocalypse was sincere, and I knew she wanted us to have the skills to survive on our own, but I didn't think she wanted to learn how to butcher any more than I did.

I didn't want to learn how to butcher. I didn't want to live in a closet with a window. I didn't want to worry about my Discman running out of batteries. I didn't want the world as we know it to end. *Don't think about that*, I told myself again.

But it was all I could think about. The coming Apocalypse was all around me—it was in the wind that rushed unabated through the trees into our cleared field, it was in the blisters on our hands and feet, it was in the blood seeped into the ground from the chicken carcasses I found every morning no matter how hard we tried to keep the foxes out. It was why we were here.

Here, in this tiny cabin we'd learned to heat, on this three-hundred-acre, off-the-grid property forty-five minutes from Smithers, in the wilderness of BC, in the middle of nowhere, where we waited for the end to come.

I tried to ignore the animals' hungry cacophony outside. It was loud but Mom still wasn't awake, so I started to twist fresh newspaper into spindles and stack it with kindling like a mini cabin, just how she taught me to. I loved the sound of the match striking the side of its box, seeing the split second where science turns to magic and fire is born of friction. No matter how many times I built a fire from scratch, seeing the tendrils of smoke curl and hearing each crack the wood makes as it burns was so satisfying. Soon, our small cabin smelled much better, as the camping-style coffee pot came to percolating life and warmth returned to the logs.

It was simple here. Not long ago, we were ordering takeout on the phone and watching TV. Now, in front of the stove, we had an ancient dining room table with a bowl of SuperValu grocery store fruit in the centre. We knew we wouldn't be able to grow our own fruit here, so we tried to get some every time we went to town; the red, orange and yellow skins added a nice burst of colour to the otherwise dark and dusty decor. The living room had one couch and one loveseat, overflowing with books. Mom must have been up all night reading sermons and the Book of Revelation again. It was close to 9:00 a.m. and still felt dark, but we were used to reading by candle or lantern light now. It was how we spent a lot of our time.

I wanted to be in the kitchen more, to learn how to live and dine like Laura Ingalls Wilder or Anne of Green Gables, but it was mainly a storage space. One of the only benefits of winter was that we could store more perishable food outside in the snow; items like milk or meat or eggs when the chickens felt like laying them were a special treat. I thanked God every day for the gravity-fed running water that also gave us an indoor toilet, and I prayed that one day I'd master the art of baking fresh bread inside a wood stove.

You won't be here much longer anyway. The intrusive thoughts returned. Thankfully, they were interrupted by Mom emerging sleepily from her bedroom. "Morning, babe. Look at you getting things done so early."

I beamed with pride, then quickly diminished it. "Well, I forgot to hide from the animals again, as you can probably hear."

Mom's cackle filled the small room easily. "They're a bunch of brats, aren't they? How was your sleep?" She poured herself a cup of coffee, and I knew what she was really asking. *Did God send you any more dreams?*

I hesitated. "I fell asleep listening to my music again, so I don't really remember. Did you read anything new last night?" I poured a packet of instant oatmeal into a bowl; I'd heat water for it in a moment.

"Yeah, ever since I started reading the Amplified version of the Bible. It sheds light on so many more things. When you pair it with the Matthew Henry commentary, it packs a wallop! Just like this coffee—thank you, babe. I think I'll do some more studying after breakfast and morning chores; what passages are you going to read today?"

I thought about my answer as I walked to the sink to fill up the kettle, but the water didn't come on. I turned the faucet again and again. Nothing.

Mom's shoulders slumped. "Oh no. Did we forget again? God, what are we doing out here?" Her voice shook with angry tears.

When the temperatures dropped drastically and we neglected to leave the faucet on a tiny bit to keep the gravity-fed spring in motion, everything in the pipes froze up. Which meant we had to add collecting snow in pots to melt on the stove for drinking water to our list of chores, an exhausting and unrewarding task as the snow always yielded half the amount of water we expected. And we had to use the outhouse.

Even though I was almost a teenager, watching my mother fall apart at the kitchen table made me feel small again.

"Mama?" I asked gently. "Are we still Spartans?"

That seemed to shake her out of what she would call her navel-gazing.

"Oh yes, babe. And you know we're even stronger because we're in God's army. We're gonna figure this out and claim this land for Him and anyone else who needs it, one day. I was just having a moment." She wiped her eyes and straightened her shoulders. "Let's go get our snow and feed those animals."

It took hours for us to melt the water we needed, and I ate a precious apple instead of instant oatmeal while I waited. Mom's words had time to turn over and over in my mind, as well as the intrusive thoughts from earlier.

They weren't new, certainly; I'd been asking Jesus to save me from Hell and from myself since I was four years old, and asking Father God to delay His judgement upon a wicked world since I was eight. But every adult

I knew had been telling me that since there was nothing I could rely on other than Heaven's finicky grace, I might as well resign myself to His will. Be wise enough to predict the approaching collapse, and harmless enough to survive it. Or, we die as martyrs for our faith. Either way, we win.

So why did it feel like a nightmare I couldn't wake up from?

I bundled myself up from head to toe in L.L. Bean gear to collect more snow. The sheep and goats happily ignored me now, eating their hay and settling in for a nap. It was cold and windy enough that a thin layer of ice had formed on top of the four-foot snow drifts, and I awkwardly braced my bulky frame into the depths so I could keep digging.

After ten scoops or so, I stopped to catch my breath. The wind bit into what little remained exposed on my face. I scanned the property in a circular motion. Across the field and frozen creek was Nick's Nest, the cabin we stayed in when we first moved up from Montana. It had two floors and a whole bathtub but ended up being too costly to keep warm for just the two of us. Now it waited silently for future occupants in need.

Between the road and our cabin were three barns. One barn was for the sheep, goats and daily-diminishing chickens. The other two were for supplies, which included two ATVs; two snowmobiles; six gasoline kegs; guns and ammo; and approximately fifty garbage bins full of rice, beans, garden seeds, clothes, tools and menstrual products.

I felt like we would never use it all and it would never be enough at the same time.

I turned my eyes back to the road and my heart leapt. I could see lights and hear the low rumble of a large vehicle. For a moment, I forgot that it was probably Dave the ploughman coming to rescue us and I believed that I saw advancing army tanks. Did they have Russian or Chinese symbols? Too far away to tell. The binoculars were inside; I picked up my snow pot and ran as quickly as one can through white concrete.

I burst through the door to see Mom smiling. "Looks like we'll make it to town this week after all!"

The adrenaline left my body in a whoosh. I set my pot on the stove and started stripping my layers off. It was barely noon and I was ready to go back to bed.

Mom bundled herself up to go greet Dave, and through the living room window I watched them chat. I wondered, did Dave ever have questions about us? Or did he just take the cash and drive? Mom never let on.

The town of Smithers usually looked like a magical snow globe village during this time of year, and I couldn't wait to see it. Not for the first time, I wished I had a camera to remember these places long after they were gone.

We had been waiting for years for Y2K; it was supposed to be any day now. Mom said it was the modern answer to biblical prophecy. Everything relied on computers now, including the creature comforts that led to our spiritual complacency, so once the computers crashed and our comforts were gone, World War III would begin. God would use it to find His true disciples, during a seven-year period called The Tribulation. Maybe He would have mercy and Rapture us to Heaven halfway through it, maybe not.

But no matter when or how it happened, America was no longer safe. This little chunk of Canadian wilderness was our best shot, no matter how much I fought thinking about it.

I had wanted to grow up and old, get married and have babies, write stories, see the world, be remembered somehow. But God and my mom knew better; they always did. I would be a witness to the end of all things, and would write down whatever I could.

Starting today.

Before Mom came back inside and saw me, I ran away from the living room window to find a pen. She was always writing notes during her studies so it didn't take long. I returned to the windowsill and paused. I'd never vandalized anything before.

Pressing down as hard as I could into the wood, I made my mark: "Carly M. Butler's SHELF ONLY."

I blew on it to make sure it dried, and then I stacked all of my books across the shelf to hide what I'd done.

I didn't want to claim this land, I just wanted this shelf. Maybe no one would ever see it, maybe it was destined to burn away.

But no one could ever say that I wasn't here.

Part One

Angels Unaware (1990–1992)

The isolation of Apocalypse began shadowing my life long before I ever knew the word.

In October of 1987, I was born to a white woman named Dorothy Jean in a California city 152 miles away from the Salton Sea, on Kizh/Tongva land, on the edge of the Sonoran Desert. From the beginning, I was always just outside of home.

Having me alone at thirty-nine had put her at some medical risk, but my mother wasn't afraid. Her doctor gave the option to have her Caesarean on October 6, 7, or 8. Mom picked 7, because it was apparently God's favourite number. All I know is it made me a Libra-Aries-Scorpio combo.

In 1990, my mom left California in a hurry, taking me to Polson, Montana. She told the locals that she had thrown her high-heeled shoes, fancy dresses and dangly earrings out the window while we drove, trading them for cowboy boots, jeans and t-shirts. Imagining her literally throwing clothes out of our vehicle always made me giggle.

We became known as the mom and daughter operating a bed and breakfast on Flathead Lake—somewhat inaccurately named for the Salish people indigenous to that area (who did not practise head mutilation like European settlers thought).

At age three, I didn't yet have any questions about the future. I didn't have any questions about miracles, either. If I had any questions at all, it might be: Can I climb this? My first memory is of the banister in my house. I had been studying it for a long time. The day I decided to climb it, I was alone, invincible in that way that toddlers believe themselves to be.

Mom was busy outside, maybe feeding the horses or cleaning a guest room. With no one to stop me, I couldn't resist straddling my legs around the handrail and giving myself a push.

I immediately tilted and fell into what I didn't realize was twelve feet of open space. I was not afraid, but I was curious about what was going to happen, like I was simply... waiting. I should have been terrified. Falling that far should have been fatal. But the pain or death that was approaching didn't seem to hold power over me like it was supposed to.

Instead, I found myself floating.

Defying gravity, I moved through the air, watching the ground slowly get closer, like I was on a cloud. No big deal. I landed on my own two feet, looked up and smiled, and carried on like this was an everyday occurrence. Looking back on my life, I'm inclined to believe it is.

I wouldn't tell my mom what happened for many years, and when I did, it was in that nonchalant way that kids have, that ability to drop tiny, universe-expanding bombs in the laps of skeptical adults.

Mom was anything but skeptical, however. She came from a long line of faith that moved mountains and entertained angels. She wouldn't be caught doubting a miracle. Her eyes widening at my words, she began a path of believing that I was special somehow, called by God, set apart for something greater.

If I'd known where it would lead us, I might have kept the story to myself.

~

In 1992, Mom sold the bed and breakfast and moved us farther northwest from Flathead Lake to Whitefish.

This area was a magnet for rich people looking to escape to their wilderness roots while still maintaining modern convenience. Whitefish, known for its lavish ski resort, fishing and fine dining was especially desirable. It was very common to hear rumours of celebrities (Wayne Gretzky, Kevin Costner, Leonardo DiCaprio, to name a few) showing interest in buying ranches nearby and disappearing when they grew tired of Hollywood life. I'm told that we saw Paula Abdul with Emilio Estevez in a bagel shop and that we had breakfast next to Jim Nabors at The Buffalo Café.

The inexplicable floating I experienced when I was three wasn't on my mind, and a world without end stretched out before me. I was living a typical childhood, just another kid of a single mom; I was happy to believe that our lives were ordinary.

She never dropped me at daycare or left me with a babysitter to go to work, and I never questioned it. Anyone else who did would get her standard reply: she would casually say something about a family inheritance and then change the subject. Determined to make her own way in the world and raise me without a man or a job, she was Ralph Lauren in a Vince Gill t-shirt. Before HGTV existed, she was drawing floor plans on graph paper and taking me on drives—what I inventively coined as "propertying"—in our old green and white Blazer to find her next renovation project. We listened to country music radio for hours, Mom and I making bets on who the artist was before the song was over. I always won.

The house my mother built for us was in the woods; it didn't have a yard, but the acreage, just twenty minutes outside of town, had an area around the house cleared of trees and full of rocks. I gallivanted all day, loosening my curly pigtails and tearing new rips in my overalls. My favourite place on the whole property was a giant boulder, and every afternoon I would climb it to have tea with Mr. Tumnus. This was, of course, after the time he was trying to fetch kids for the White Witch of Narnia; he was nice now and I was safe.

Mom was my safe place too. Every morning, I could count on her to move over in her bed for a snuggle, as long as I didn't toss and turn. She always tried to sing me back to sleep with *I love you, a bushel and a peck, a bushel and a peck, and a hug around the neck*... but I never did. I just listened to her voice.

~

I loved listening to her voice. And I wasn't the only one. A decade before I had ears to hear it, she made two vinyl albums full of biblical lyrics, and one song, "I Will Change Your Name," became very well known. My mom had always been passionate about her faith. Born to missionary parents overseas, she was raised strictly Southern Baptist in Florida, but she was free to go wherever the wind whisked her—for the glory of the Gospel, community and connection. In 1963, at the age of fifteen, she drove herself to Alberta to finish her adolescent education at Prairie Bible Institute. By 1976, at the age of twenty-seven, she graduated from the University of Georgia as a Licensed Clinical Social Worker.

Not long afterwards, she moved to southern California to set up her practice. During the week, she counselled patients in a clinic with spiritual guidance, and on Sundays she led worship at the local Vineyard congregation, a passionate new "Jesus movement" that was very different from the conservative Southern Baptism with which she had grown up. The Vineyard showed her a charismatic way, a faith of big emotions and dreams and prophecies and tongues spoken that only Spirit and a select few people could understand.

Falling in love with this fresh Holy Spirit inspired her songwriting for the next five years, the wind whisking her as far as Europe for a church tour in 1980 after the release of her second album.

After she returned home to California, she also began falling in love with my father, but it would be a long time before I would understand who he was to her, or to me.

Now, it was 1992 and I wasn't worried about that. It was just me, and Mom, her voice singing to me in the mornings, and our new home.

We lived happily in this house created from Mom's mind, combined from a demolished 1900s farmhouse and blacksmith shop, miles away. We knew this because we found newspaper "insulation" in the walls with the date 1914 on them—which is the year after my grandmother was born. I think Mom felt like it was a little greeting from Heaven, and I tried to imagine another family member I'd never meet. I can still remember the silty smell of the ink and dirt.

My five-year-old world consisted of my Narnia boulder, a narrow brook depending on rainfall, and a grove of trees I longed to explore if it weren't so dark. I didn't know that the Kootenai, Pend d'Oreille, and Bitterroot Salish tribes had been able to keep this land to themselves right up until the late 1800s. I didn't know anything.

~

One day while I played Narnia as usual, the local police showed up at our door. They asked to see my birth certificate. My mom complied, though she was obviously upset.

"As you can see, Carly is mine. She looks a lot like her father and he's not around, that's all." She kept her cool long enough to send them away satisfied, but said to friends later, "That was none of their damn business. Government interference is getting out of control, isn't it? I can't believe I pay taxes for this."

I wouldn't understand for a long time that there had been multiple incidents of kidnapping from the local reservation, and someone in town had observed that my mom was white, while I was not.

They had to ask. One day, I would too.

Mom fancied herself to be like a pioneer of old, seeking out new frontiers and shunning a lot of modern conveniences in favour of the "old fashioned." All our furniture and decor was thrifted from antique stores and pawn shops, and while it felt completely normal to me, anyone who visited our home might feel like they had stepped back in time. Tiffany stained glass lamps, elaborately framed mirrors, leather-bound trunks acting as coffee tables, ornate solid wood wardrobes and four-poster rope beds were just a few of the valuable items in our daily use.

I think it reminded Mom of the ancestors she'd always heard about. "Your great-granddaddy, John G. McCrory—yes, McCrory, just like your middle name—was a visionary. He brought his family over from England almost one hundred years ago with next to nothing, and he bought the land across the river from New York City on purpose because he knew that one day they'd have to build a bridge there. Well, sure enough, they did; John G. made a lot of money off that land so he could start his five-and-dime business, and people still drive over the George Washington Bridge to this day."

She took pride in making sure I was interested in the stories of strong girls. Anne of Green Gables, Laura Ingalls Wilder, the American Girl book series—but she also didn't want me reading all day. She, like her grandfather, had a vision for this place, and she wanted me to see it.

To spruce the yard up and teach me the value of a good work ethic, Mom had me plant two hundred purple petunias in front of the house. I hated every moment, but the lesson was learned when the vision of the beautiful yard came together, and I received a long-desired American Girl doll, Addy Walker, for my birthday later that year.

Mom had been confused when I asked her. "Are you sure she's the one you want?"

Well, obviously I wanted all of them, but I wanted Addy first. I had started attending kindergarten at a private Christian school and I'd already been fed lines like "separate but equal" and "the Civil War was about states' rights," so I somehow completely filed the story of Addy's escape from slavery into the "alternate universe" category. Sure, all of the American Girls had overcome obstacles, but the way Addy's family started a new life for themselves against all odds enthralled me; I wanted to be like her. Much like the petunias, knowing her story planted something within my character that would bloom later.

As part of the move to Montana, and continuing her lifelong curiosity about different congregations, Mom began searching for the "right" church for us. First, there was Alliance. Then Foursquare. Then Presbyterian, because of a well-known charismatic pastor named Jack Deere, who was a friend of Mom's well-known Vineyard pastor John Wimber. I was six and we had been living in the Beaver Lake House for almost two years when the Pentecostal Church congregation we'd been a part of split. We followed the small group who believed they wanted to see Jesus change lives in a new way, and now we met in a gym. This is when Mom started writing songs again, but somewhere along the way the lyrics underwent a tonal shift. Instead of the loneliness-defying love of God she sang about in "I Will Change Your Name," her new songs spoke of spiritual domination: "This is war, this is war / Shoulder to shoulder, we love taking new land! / This is war, this is war / Lion of Judah, teach us how to roar! / Some heads are gonna roll..."

Every Sunday, I expressed my love of Heaven by waving flags and dancing when the service started, and counteracted my fear of Hell by saying the Sinner's Prayer by the time the service ended. The Sinner's Prayer was as simple as the ABCs I'd already learned to identify by age four: accept, believe, confess.

Accept that you are a wretched sinner. Believe that Jesus died for you. Confess your sins and be forgiven.

And D: defeat the Devil. I didn't know why he wanted me so badly, but I was determined to fight him every step of the way.

~

I enjoyed our new gym church, but truly, for me, Bible study is where it was at. We joined two different home groups, and even though I was forced to take a nap like a *baby* so we could stay out late, it was always worth it.

At my favourite house, the mom made a bowl of popcorn bigger than my whole body and sent us kids into a *second* living room to watch *Star Wars* and *Grease* on LaserDisc until we passed out. My other favourite house had not one, not two, but *three* golden retrievers, who looked just like Shadow from *Homeward Bound*.

The adults would talk for hours about prophecies and miracles and a violent future that sat like a rock in my stomach no matter how hard I tried to ignore it by distracting myself with the TV. Mom's favourite stories were of gold dust appearing on people's hands as they worshipped and angel sightings in the form of "hitchhikers" that gave an important message to the driver before disappearing. "Hebrews says we entertain angels unaware! And I'm gonna find one," she declared with excitement in her voice.

I didn't know what angels were supposed to look like, but I felt like I would just know one when I saw them. Like a "God thing," as Mom called it.

One summer Sunday night between kindergarten and grade one, Mom and I attended a church meeting at a public park, instead of at the gym as usual. The park was mostly an open field, with a small grove of trees and gazebo along the Whitefish River, and I was certain I saw an angel nearby. This stranger was wearing white flowy clothes and doing movements barefoot in the grass while our worship leader played his guitar—not unlike the way I would dance with a flag at the altar on a Sunday morning. If anyone *looked* like an angel, surely this person did.

I interrupted Mom's prayer time to tell her and she excitedly let me lead her through the park to witness her miracle. When I pointed them out Mom had a mixed expression of amused disappointment. "Oh, Carly-Belle," she said, using her favourite nickname for me, "That person is just doing yoga or tai chi, something like that. Definitely not an angel. But you were right to let me know; keep looking."

I felt foolish. After being so certain only to be met with being wrong, after confusing something profane for something holy, I didn't keep looking. My intuition was clearly faulty; someone from Heaven above would have to appear to me glowing with a sword for me to believe now.

I kept reading my Bible and praying, though. I watched *VeggieTales* and *Superbook* (a safe, biblical anime alternative to *Pokémon*), and every

Good Friday, I'd watch a pale Son of God with blue eyes get whipped and nailed to the cross, no matter how much I wished he wouldn't. Every day I worried that maybe I'd done something to undo my salvation, so I gave my heart to Jesus every night before bed. At the same time, I vowed that one day, I would have a LaserDisc player and a golden retriever of my own. *Just* one, though. Three made me tired after a while.

Thinking about possible names for this future dog was a lot more pleasant than the grown-up whispers that were getting harder to ignore.

Social Butterfly (1992–1995)

We first moved to Whitefish in 1992 and it took six months for my mom and her contractors to finish work on the Beaver Lake House. Living there was one of the few times we had cable TV, and I remember being forced to eat granola on natural yogurt every morning while the news told us what President Bill Clinton had said or done the day before. I didn't understand what was happening, but based on Mom's body language and verbal muttering, it didn't seem like a relaxing way to start the day. She enjoyed Pat Robertson, the 700 Club, and Jack Van Impe Ministries much more. I escaped their voices through my books, only really paying attention briefly again much later when JonBenét Ramsey and Princess Diana died.

By the time Mom was feeling the itch to start another project for us to live in, it was 1994 and I was getting ready to start first grade. My school was in town and the commute from our house became too strenuous, so Mom found a fixer-upper, a rancher on Dakota Avenue. It was in a developing neighbourhood a mere bike ride from Whitefish Lake; Mom had her team of contractors turn the two-car garage into a giant living room and build me a playhouse in the backyard to ease the pain of transition. It wasn't Mr. Tumnus's boulder, but it would do.

~

I wanted to love school because I loved being around people, but truthfully, it was only tolerable because of creative writing and recess. The writing part came naturally to me, and recess was for attempting athleticism: chasing boys I liked, climbing, swimming, and reaching beyond my paygrade to be included in the activities of Cool Girls. They had no intention of ever actually including me, but they sure liked to dangle carrots. The mere fact I was attending Cross Currents Christian School meant they knew that I had money, which I think garnered me some acceptability, but I also had no dad and I liked to hum loudly while I wrote my assignments. I tried too hard to make others laugh with my antics, which was more annoying than cool. Plus, my skin was darker than everyone else's. My head was covered with wild black curls (minus an inexplicable bald spot on each side of my head since birth) and full of too many teeth. I created mystery stories and did not seem to notice that changing after swimming lessons meant that, for a moment at least, I was *naked* in front of everyone. I didn't understand why I had to ask permission to use the bathroom, or why my grade one teacher Miss Nelson told my mom to make sure I recited the Pledge of Allegiance correctly.

I was weird, and they made me feel badly about it.

The only girl who let me in with no strings attached was Catie. She was new to our class and she didn't fit in either—she had cerebral palsy and our playground was too hilly for her canes to navigate, so she spent most of her free time sitting on the floor or ground playing pretend. Since I was an only child, this was *also* one of my favourite things to do. We discovered that we liked to be puppies or kitties, but our true love was being horses. No one thought their teeth were too big or their legs were too crooked—they just ran wild and free. We bucked and neighed awkwardly, laughing until we couldn't breathe.

I didn't realize that my body was a little bit different too. I was used to feeling like my feet were too small to support the rest of me, used to tripping or losing my balance or being decorated with bruises. There were so many things I wanted to do with my body, like ride horses and play soccer and do gymnastics. Those were things I could *picture* my body doing; I think the common denominator was physical freedom that could be witnessed. No one really cared when I lost myself in a book for hours, but certainly they could cheer for me in a field or a gym.

But my body never got the memo. Every day my brain would tell my limbs to move this way or that, and sometimes they just wouldn't. Or they would, but much slower than required. It was like my whole network was one of those old-style strings of Christmas lights that wouldn't work if one bulb was blown somewhere, but I had no idea which bulb it was or why.

I enjoyed horseback riding, soccer and gymnastics while it lasted, but I was constantly losing my balance, losing the reins, losing the ball. Mom was a little concerned. She told me that when I was learning to walk, I was constantly running into walls, so I had a brain MRI.

"The doctors said it was the most unique MRI they'd ever seen," Mom said, "and they asked permission to send it to specialists in Boston. I said they could, and then I never heard back from them."

Maybe what she meant was we had unexpectedly left town. Or maybe the MRI had been unremarkable after all.

I was put in a gentle callisthenics class with Catie and a few other kids during school lunchtime, and got participation ribbons on Sports Days—beaming the whole day after I got a "Most Improved" ribbon.

I wondered, to Mom's excitement, if maybe I was meant for more traditional activities like baking. She bought me, her "little homesteader," a Betty Crocker's Cooking CD-ROM and gave up some of her daily computer study time so that I could use it. She respected those skills, but disdained them personally. She had been working for herself for less than a decade, but she was good at building kitchens, not cooking in them.

She would much rather take me and my friends to Jimmy Lee's for Chinese food on Friday nights, and the Buffalo Café for brunch after church on Sundays. I loved the buttered noodles and French toast the size of my face, but my personal favourite day was Wednesday: I'd fumble my way through gymnastics in a mall studio directly after school, and then we'd walk a few units over to Little Italy, a hole-in-the-wall diner that had maybe ten red-and-white-check gingham-draped tables in it altogether. To light the whole room, each table featured a centrepiece of a candle tucked into a glass bottle covered with wood strips that was draped in about a dozen different colours of wax, telling years of stories in flames gone by.

Little Italy was run by Rosa and her husband Emilio. Even though it was always busy, Rosa's shadow as animated as the paintings of the Italian countryside on the walls, she never forgot what I wanted: Emilio's famous spaghetti followed by a dish of spumoni ice cream. It was maybe the only "weird" item my palate enjoyed; something about the combination of chocolate brown, black-cherry red and pistachio green swirled together worked for me, and I felt like an internationally travelled adult every time I ordered it.

After Little Italy, we'd drive straight to the Alliance church for Awana Club, which was like Scouts for church kids, but co-ed, and I used every bit of that spaghetti and spumoni to fuel my memory for Bible verses, songs, and tips for evangelizing my friends. I wanted the achievement badges for my vest.

We would enjoy our lives this way all through the winter, like we were in hibernation mode. And then inevitably every spring, Mom would go through a phase where we stopped going to restaurants and she would throw out every single food item with white flour or white sugar, replacing it with dried fruit and large glass jars of mushroom tea. My mouth still puckers and my nose twitches when I think about those billowing fungi fermenting into a sludge that permeated the whole room even though the jar was tightly sealed.

Brown bread and brown sugar were even suspect, likely just white flour and sugar dyed with molasses. "I keep reading online about new ways the government is trying to poison us, slow us down," she said.

Maybe they were, but I'd rather take my chances than bring cartons of beet juice and bags of trail mix to school. I wanted to bake bread pudding and have a dishwasher while Mom fantasized about hanging apple slices from ceiling strings in a log cabin kitchen far away.

~

Aside from hanging out with Catie, and burying myself in my creative writing assignments, I mostly measured school out by holidays. Fridays had morning chapel in a separate building, so we got to go for a walk *and* I could sing as loud as I wanted. My favourite songs were about being in the Lord's Army and shining the light of Jesus wherever I went.

Octobers were not for Halloween but, instead, a harvest party, and we dressed up as our favourite Bible characters. Sometimes I chose Ruth and sometimes I chose Esther, for the same reason: in them, I saw that after you go to that new place God tells you to—to save your family and the lives of others—you fall in love and live happily ever after.

Novembers were for Thanksgiving, a time for making paper turkeys out of our hand tracings and decorating paper bags to make vests for the "Pilgrims & Indians" pageant, complete with large feathers for our hair. Mom gushed over the class pictures with her "Yaqui Indian princess" and when I asked her what that meant, her face went even paler for a moment with regret. "Your daddy was a Yaqui Indian man, he told me once. I figure that makes you a Yaqui Indian too."

Decembers used to be for Christmas until Mom did research on our computer with something called the internet and discovered that it was actually a pagan holiday. No more trees or presents or traditions that might pay homage to idolatry and offend God. Still, I caused a stir at the school Christmas concert by wearing makeup and shoving the boy in front of me off the stage after he wouldn't stop swaying back and forth during "Away in a Manger."

February featured Valentine's Day, and our desks had little mailboxes attached to the front and everyone was required to make a Valentine for each classmate, so no one got left out. It didn't always get enforced.

If you didn't wear green on St. Patrick's Day, you literally got pinched. But we ate real green eggs and ham.

Easter was especially about Jesus and how we caused his horribly painful death but neither we nor the Devil could stop him. But also, there were calla lilies. I was often presented with the Big Important Things that adults wanted me to care about—like sin and redemption—but so often it was the little things that I noticed the most, that I cared most about: like the very faint scent of calla lilies in the chapel during Easter vigil, or the taste of the green eggs and ham we got to eat on St. Patrick's Day, or the sound of mine and Catie's voices in chapel. Our favourite song was a rousing rendition of "Oil in My Lamp":

Give me oil in my lamp, keep me burning!
Give me oil in my lamp I pray, hallelujah!
Give me oil in my lamp, keep me burning!
Keep me burning till the break of day!

Just before school let out in May, we would commemorate both Mother's and Father's Day with special crafts for the parents in our lives. I always used Father's Day to catch up on my reading.

And birthday parties were all year round, hallelujah.

This was my normal. Well, as normal as life could be for a kid in a Christian school, a kid with only a mom and no dad at home, a kid whose body didn't know she had undiagnosed dyspraxia, a kid who was paying attention. It was normal to me because I was living it.

Jessica (1995)

My friend Jessica was only ten years old the day she died. I'm the only one who saw it happen.

It was summer 1995. I was soaking up all the lake days with my friends that I could, but there was one particular, *special*, day that I was looking forward to: Swimming Pool on the Mountain Day. I had just finished first grade with Catie, and now that we could go over to each other's houses more, I also became good friends with her sister, Jessica. Their mom, Dawn, had made plans to attend an evangelical women's conference and invited my mom to come with her; the hotel that was hosting the event was at the ski resort on Big Mountain, and had its own pool. It was one of the fanciest things I could think of, and Jessica was going to spend the whole day swimming with me there. I don't remember what Catie's plans were; I just remember being sad that there was no accessible way for her to join us.

Jessica was older than us by three years, but she didn't seem to notice. She had gloriously long caramel-brown hair and loved to swim like I did. She was second only to Ariel as the mermaid queen of my heart.

On the drive up to the resort, I could barely think of anything except my own excitement and impatience about the day's adventures with Jessica. We sat in the back of the minivan reading our books, and as we drove I overheard Dawn tell my mom that she'd had a dream the previous night that shook her to the core. "I think the Devil is after my kids." Mom was always eager to talk about dreams and their meanings, so they talked and prayed animatedly for the rest of the drive and, as always, I tuned it out. Usually halfway into a mountain drive, I would ask for a piece of chewing gum to make my ears pop so I could hear again. This time, I just looked out the window and let all sound drift slowly away. The sun and blue sky were sparkling through the trees; I didn't think anything could darken the day.

Since it was the less busy off-season, we were able to find parking quickly. The main lodge looked almost foreboding, framed with dark logs and braced by huge river rocks. We were only a few miles out of town, but it felt like the middle of nowhere. My ears started to pop.

Mom and Dawn showed us where their conference room was and then walked us down to the pool area. It wasn't far, maybe a few hallways over. They said they would come pick us up around three o'clock in the afternoon; it was almost eleven in the morning when they left.

We quickly got changed and entered the pool area. The first thing I noticed was that we were completely alone. No guests, no lifeguards. But we were strong swimmers, and having a whole pool and hot tub to ourselves was the stuff of dreams.

We played and splashed and laughed for hours, alternating between the big pool and the hot tub. I never wanted the afternoon to end. I kept my eye on the clock, knowing how many minutes were cruelly creeping by until our moms picked us up.

Our skin was starting to wrinkle and I was getting cold.

"Let's go in the hot tub one last time to warm up!" Jessica said.

"Okay! Wanna play the hold-your-breath game?" I replied.

She smiled. It was a competition we'd been engaged in all afternoon. One turn at a time, dunking under, the other person watching the clock to count the seconds. We averaged between thirty and forty seconds each time; one minute was the goal we'd never achieved.

She dunked, and then I did. She dunked again, and then I did. She was determined to beat me the third time. I counted the seconds on the clock. When she passed thirty-five seconds, I knew she would win. Forty... forty-five... was she going to seize the one-minute winner-takes-all prize?

People often say when a life-changing trauma occurs that "everything happened so fast." For me, it was the exact opposite. The seconds crawled by like snails and she was still under the bubbles. Despite a pit in my stomach that said something was wrong, I laughed and said, "Okay, okay, you win! You can come up now."

Maybe she didn't hear me. Almost two minutes. I reached into the water to tap on her head.

Nothing.

I grabbed her shoulder and started shaking her. She was stuck.

"Jessica! JESSICA!" I started screaming and glancing around. As had been the case all afternoon, no one was there.

Suddenly, her body bobbed to the surface, but her head was still down in the water, and I couldn't pull her out.

I don't understand. What is happening? Why won't she come back?

I fled the hot tub, determined to find help. I reached the door, opened it and stopped in my tracks.

Carpet. Nice, clean, fancy carpet. And there I was, dripping wet, remembering that I'd been told to never step on anyone's carpet when I was wet. Mould would grow underneath, and the carpet would be ruined.

This thought kept me from running any farther. So I stood at the doorway, calling out over and over, even though I could see no one. Someone had to hear me.

I'm alone. It's all up to me. God, please send someone. Anyone!

In desperation, I ran back into the hot tub, and tried with all my strength to remove Jessica from it. I heard my screams echo off the tiles.

It felt like hours. It felt like being abandoned. It felt like I was watching a movie of this scenario happening to someone else. It felt like it was all my fault. But there was a tiny part of me that was sure she was going to pop out of the water like a fish any second now with a smile on her face, declaring herself the winner of the game for all time.

SLAM! The door burst open, and a man ran in, like a guardian angel who'd gotten caught in traffic.

"What happened?" He had dark hair and a strong build, but even he strained to free her.

I froze, my words pouring out slowly. "We were playing... a game... she was holding her breath... and... she never came up." Would this angel blame me?

"Okay, honey. I'm gonna go get some help. Are you okay here for a minute?"

I nodded. What was one more minute?

I never left her side. I started to shake. I thought I was cold, but shock had also begun to set in.

The door opened again, this time with six giant, too-late guardian angels to help me. I sat on the edge of the hot tub, curled up with my arms wrapped around my knees as they suctioned to the bodice of my swimsuit.

I had no concept of the time anymore.

It took all six of them to finally bring her limp body out of the water. Her princess hair covered her face, and as they laid her down on the concrete, one of them began CPR, sweeping the hair away. She was light blue.

That's when I knew this wasn't a movie I was watching. It was happening to me. I remember the helicopter that took her away and the gravel that bit my wrinkled feet as I walked across the parking lot, covered in a blanket. That's where my mom found me and scooped me up in her arms. I never saw Jessica or her mom again.

Later, at the hospital, doctors confirmed what we already knew. Jessica's hair, that I'd wanted so badly, had gotten sucked into a filter at the bottom of the tub.

Nobody asked me what happened. Not the hospital, not my mom, not a pastor or a therapist. I was never asked, so I never said anything. I think my mom believed that her psychiatry training would send off any red flags if I was in trouble.

In the days that followed, I replayed everything in my mind, trying to think if I could've changed the outcome by doing something different. I kept coming back to the carpet and my fear of getting in trouble for making it wet.

Screw the carpet. I should have run until I found a person, I should have found a phone and called 9-1-1, I should have....

It brought slight relief to my mind when Jessica's parents learned that the hotel had been remiss in their maintenance of the hot tub to begin with, and the emergency shut-off valve had been located behind a locked iron door. They used their grief to pursue legal avenues to make sure that hot tubs and their filters were made differently; I used mine to internalize that dreams were warnings, and to keep my hair short.

And still I wondered: In an emergency, in a life-or-death situation, was I capable of saving anyone? Was this God's will or was I a weak link, a soft spot for Death and the Devil to have their way, knowing they could get away with it?

My Body Is Not My Own (1995–1996)

It turns out that even when you watch one of your friends drown in front of you in August, you still must go back to school in September.

All my classmates heard what had happened, and they became more distant than ever. Catie had left our school, and I felt her absence deeply. I didn't know how to apologize for being the last person to see her sister alive, and even if she had stayed, there was no going back to our carefree animal games. Miss Erisman, my grade two teacher, took me under her wing a bit, and she convinced me that maybe it was all right to smile again every once in a while.

She was single and had a ferret; I stayed the weekend at her apartment when my mom went to Florida for a McCrory Family Business trip. We ordered pizza and gathered up on the couch with the ferret while watching Disney movies. When my mom returned, I almost didn't want to leave.

Eventually my class forgot that I was the kid who had seen Death. The boys got older and meaner and unfortunately this was when the girls realized they could not beat them, so they joined them. Mom told me if I didn't stand up to them, people like that would "lead me around by the nose" for the rest of my life, but I never could bring myself to do it.

This was never more evident than with the girls in my neighbourhood, Jackie and Cara.

We rode our bikes everywhere, and to keep us busy Mom gave me money for snacks and VHS rentals at the nearby mart. She never noticed that we were sneaking films above a PG rating (*Now and Then* and *Forrest Gump* were frequent flyers); she also never noticed that I kept the change every single time she gave me money. I would add every leftover dollar to a glass jar on my bookshelf when I got home. I wasn't trying to be deceitful; she had just never clarified that it wasn't mine. I was truly confused at her anger the day she found my "piggy bank"; and then, in trying to stand up for myself like I thought she wanted, I was received as a rebellious back-talker.

I quickly discovered that I hated the feeling of misunderstanding someone or being misunderstood myself.

I stopped stealing and backtalking and renting inappropriate movies after Mom took me to the hardware store and made me pick out my own cutting board with a handle. I had always done my best to be good in order to avoid a spank from her hand, but now I was older and appeared to need more motivation. Shame made my legs feel like Jell-O as I browsed the kitchenware aisles, certain that the store employees must know why I was here.

Being raised by Mom was like being raised by God: I knew they loved me, and my love walked in step with my dread of their correction. Mom was still determined to raise me by herself, and her 1950s Southern Baptist upbringing of "breaking a child's will but not their spirit" didn't appear broken, so she didn't see a need to fix it. She believed God had given me to her to be trained, like the quarter-horses she used to ride back in her Georgia college days. She said that discipline now would save me from Hell later and that's what I wanted more than anything.

In a world determined to snatch my soul from God's hand, I let the possibility of pain make me feel safer.

"A thinner board will actually hurt more," Mom said, as if testing to see if I had any rebellion left.

The cutting board stayed tucked between Mom's mattress and box spring; it didn't come out very often, I made sure of that. Whether by will or exceptional secrecy, I began creating a persona of piety that would serve me until I was considered too old to threaten with wood. Any secret rebellion I did have left was kept alive by Jackie and Cara. They weren't from our church or my Christian school. Their families indulged in worldly enjoyments that would bring God's judgement and this made them risky to be around. But reaching other people for Jesus without spending any time with them didn't make sense to me. Maybe, if they were really my friends like I hoped they were, I could invite them to Awana Club or Sunday school and they would come, their souls would be saved and God would see that I was trustworthy.

Unfortunately, they were just so tempting with their cool clothes and bright smiles and modern toys. I knew that I needed to be careful, but I never really understood why I wasn't allowed to have a Barbie doll or a Nintendo, so spending time at Jackie or Cara's house made me want to play with their Barbies and Nintendos all the more. Instead of inviting them to church, I was yell-singing songs from the *Clueless* soundtrack or Gwen Stefani and No Doubt's *Tragic Kingdom* album. Instead of introducing them to Bible verses, we conquered Bowser and made Ken and Barbie fall in love.

My friends laughed at my wide eyes when they started taking off Barbie and Ken's clothes while making them kiss. "They're married, now they're going to have sex!" And the story would continue.

I learned what sex was from them, and movies, extremely incorrectly. I would go home and tell Mom what new word I had learned that day, and she would just laugh, brushing it off. She said I could ask her anything, but I was fairly confident I already knew the answers. A mix of embarrassment and shame kept me from ever coming back to the questions.

As kids often do, we got bored with our Barbie and Ken storyline. The whole dynamic changed when Jackie said she'd found a book her parents kept hidden, with pictures of actual people having real sex in them. It looked fun, and she could show us how.

And so the story evolved. Now *we* were Barbie and Ken: meeting, falling in love, hanging out and using swear words for absolutely no reason other than they tasted good on our lips, and eventually, taking off our clothes and exploring.

I was usually deemed the "Ken" of the group, and I didn't like it but I didn't say anything because I was finally in with the Cool Girl group. After years of being seen as the weird kid that nobody could quite put a label on, I already understood that if I didn't play my role, I would be left out. And to me, there was nothing worse than that.

We never took off our underwear, and we never actually kissed. Those were the only rules. We could say whatever scandalous thing we could think of, and then we would tuck our lips inside our teeth and "make out." Tangled in each other's arms and hair, rolling around beds, trying to be quiet so a mom wouldn't come barging in. Sometimes, I can still smell the sweat another girl imprinted on my skin. Afterwards, I wondered why my underwear seemed damp, my belly tingling.

It wasn't long before all of our regular play was replaced with this. Playdates, sleepovers—it all ended in fake heteronormative lovemaking that I couldn't quit, no matter how many times I prayed that Jesus would help me suggest going back to Nintendo next time.

When I was alone in my bed, I discovered that a pillow made a pretty decent replacement. Maybe it was okay for me to do this, as long as I didn't involve anyone else, didn't fate anyone else to be stained by my guilt. Surely, I was the only one who had discovered this feeling, this secret, this shame.

God, it felt so good to move my tiny hips back and forth. God, I'm sorry. God, I loved kissing that pillow. God, forgive me. Again.

I shut down my body completely not long after that. I could no longer breathe through the guilt of what I'd been doing in secret, so I told my mom. I expected the wooden cutting board with a handle to make an appearance, but instead, I received common ground.

"I think every kid gets curious about their body and their friends' bodies at some point; I know I did. It's just important to know that your body was created by God, so it belongs to God. We are the temple of His Spirit so we must do our best to keep it holy and ask forgiveness when we don't. Does that make sense?"

I nodded. No longer tuning out things I didn't want to hear, I started paying attention during church and Bible study. I'd been trying to do everything my own way and, naturally, everything had turned into a sinful mess. Every Sunday morning sermon was getting heavier, and I only found release when I wept at the altar. I had been making appeals like this at every church camp, chapel and church service since I knew how to form words... but now, the stakes were too high. Following pleasures of the flesh led to boys kissing other boys, and girls killing their babies after they kissed boys. We were getting radical, marching in the streets to declare Jesus's name and hope that people heard and called for mercy. God's judgement was approaching and cultural complacency would be set ablaze. Pleasure was not worth the pain.

My body was not my own. Sensual stimulus in any form was off the table until I got married—to a man, of course. If I lived long enough to get married, my husband would get all of me.

The End Is Near (1996–1997)

By the time grade two ended and the summer of 1996 rolled around, Mom had gotten bored with the Dakota Avenue rancher. In a move that was completely out of character, she chose a brand new house in a brand new cul-de-sac just across the highway from Dakota Avenue. She was approaching her late forties now, only stopping her daily internet studies to take a nap; maybe she just needed a break. The Crestwood Court house had three storeys, three bedrooms, two bathrooms, and one blessed dishwasher.

Even though I was starting to hate moving, putting some distance between me and Jackie and Cara came as a relief. We still found time to ride our bikes and go to the lake, but I kept the sleepovers to a minimum. When summer ended and our different schools began, we naturally went our separate ways.

I wanted to focus on Jesus, on making my mom proud of me, on reading enough Nancy Drew books to write my own mysteries and playing with my Addy Walker American Girl.

I knew that I had a lot to be grateful for. For as long as I could remember, every night before bed, Mom would cup her hands over her mouth, breathe in and out a few times, and then place her hands over my heart. As I felt the heat seep in, she'd sing an old hymn that her mother used to sing to her:

Safe am I, safe am I
In the hollow of His Hand
Sheltered o'er, sheltered o'er
In His Love forevermore
No ill can harm me, no foe alarm me
For He keeps both day and night
Safe am I, safe am I
In the hollow of His Hand.

And then she'd smile. "There. Now your bucket is a little fuller. I love you, babe, sleep well." I would tuck into her warmth and pray that my dreams would be sweet. I was safe. My mom loved me. I was going into grade three, I had survived the loss of Jessica, and broken the influence of Cara and Jackie on my weak heart. I was following the right path to Jesus. All was well.

But by early 1997, in the middle of my third-grade spring break, it was clear that all was not well.

One morning, I awoke to Mom sitting on the edge of my bed with a serious look on her face. I was immediately uneasy, because for every single morning before this one, I was always the one to leave my bed and crawl into hers while she woke up.

"Carly... you know that, for a while now, I've been reading what people around the world are saying about the future. The more I read... wow... the more I feel sure that something bad is coming down the pike, and I think you're ready to know because we need to be ready together. You remember the Bible talks about the end times and Jesus's return... well, it's coming."

The hellfire sermons, the hushed conversations at Bible study, the long prayer meetings, the daily news... every grown-up thing I had spent so much effort to tune out could no longer be ignored. Suddenly, my room felt like it was shrinking, along with my lungs. I had dedicated myself, body and soul, to Jesus Christ just in time.

"It's called Y2K, and it's going to end the world on the first of January, the year 2000. Computers aren't going to work anymore, governments are going to fall, we're going to see military takeover from other countries. So, I think God wants me to take you out of school when you're done this year. He told me to set you apart, that you'll be just like everyone else if you stay there. We can still see your friends for as long we can, but you'll be starting fourth grade at home, okay?"

I swallowed hard and did not protest. It seemed pretty set in stone by God already, so what was the point in arguing? There were only a few friends I would actually miss, and it's not like I was *never* going to see them again. Besides, there were still two and a half years left before Y2K.

I finished third grade at Cross Currents Christian School and never went back. I had no way of knowing it would be another ten years before I set foot in a classroom again.

We spent the summer of 1997 shopping for strictly Christian curriculum Abeka workbooks in Math, English, History and Science that I could do at home—although Mom maintained that the most important things I learned were "Readin', Writin', and 'Rithmetic."

I *hated* 'rithmetic with a burning passion. Adding, subtracting, multiplying, dividing and fractions made sense to me, I saw it play out in music theory, money and baking. But once the textbook started replacing my tried-and-true numbers with letters, my brain would immediately get overwhelmed and shut down.

I don't think Mom and I ever fought more than we did over the subject of math. She had been counting on my previous motivation as a "self-starter" to carry over into my work at home, so that she could continue her internet studies uninterrupted. But I needed help, and sometimes, the back of the book gave me just that.

Now that I was out of school, we traded checkups and vaccinations for a naturopath who told me that my brown eyes were actually blue underneath all the toxins I was consuming. I tried to imagine how beautiful I would be with blue eyes instead, but I missed my Cool Ranch Doritos and Dr Pepper too much.

Mom did further research and discovered an updated cavity prevention procedure called dental sealants, which is a liquid plastic that gets painted onto the surface of each tooth. It wasn't fully known if they were safe yet, and they usually weren't meant for adults. But somehow, she found a dentist willing to put the sealants on our teeth to prevent decay for as long as possible.

After our first appointment, he said I needed braces, and I would've liked them, but Mom painted a terrifying scenario after we left: "I know your teeth give you trouble, but it's not a good idea. I don't want to pay all that money just for World War III to start and have no one available to remove that metal from your mouth. Braces forever, can you imagine?"

I was barely ten, so yeah, I could. No, thank you. Sealants would have to suffice.

We went back a second time to finish putting our sealants on. It was awkward lying in the dentist chair with a bright light shining in my face, listening to my mom dance around the reasons why we were here, without getting braces. She chalked it up to lack of money, which was a blatant lie. Mom had already prepared me to be silent, and that lying for a greater godly purpose was sometimes required.

"Well, you both should be good for the next few years now," our dentist said. "Just promise me you'll find a way to get braces on those teeth by the time she's a teenager."

"You got it," Mom said.

My new teeth tasted odd, and I wondered how long the sealants would last, where I would be when they wore off. Were they to be swallowed? What about my adult teeth that hadn't even come in yet?

The world is ending in two years; you'll be with the Lord long before it becomes an issue, an inner voice rationalized.

We spent an inordinate amount of time in Costco and pawn shops. Mom believed that when Y2K started, modern conveniences like computers and credit and paper money would become worthless. So she cut up all her credit cards, took all her money out of the bank, and started investing her McCrory family inheritance in authentic gold and silver coins. I would wander around the dark, musty pawn shop, not touching anything while she dickered with the owner over what was going to be most valuable in a crisis. She also started stocking our pantry up with bags of rice and beans and other non-perishables; we would leave Costco with pallets weekly.

During church at the gym one Sunday, one of our leaders told us about a new music video by the popular Christian singer Ray Boltz. He had been making waves with *I Pledge Allegiance to the Lamb*, which depicted a father telling his son about Christians throughout history who had been martyred for their faith. Mom and I wept as we saw our fellow believers stoned to death, burned at the stake, and held at gunpoint.

I was shocked by the ending when we realized that this father and son had been in a detention camp the whole time. "I hope that you're never put in the position that you have to choose between your faith and your life. But if you are, I know which choice you're gonna make, because I know that

Jesus lives inside of you. In the meantime, just pray like I taught you how to, and take care of your mom, and remember that God is the Father of the fatherless," the man said, weeping as the police took him away.

Mom felt certain this would be our fate too. She said the music video was simply missing our guillotines that were secretly being imported from the other side of the world on trains. I thought about how many ways there were to die, and I hoped for the least painful one. I felt like a coward for hoping that.

On weekend nights, we would go to Blockbuster and rent movies with a PG-thirteen (or higher) rating, which was okay as long as they had themes of war and violence and government takeover and survival. *Deep Impact*, *Braveheart*, *The Postman*, *The Hiding Place*, just to name a few. She said she wanted me to get used to seeing horrific things so that I wouldn't lose my shit when I saw it in real life.

But nudity was forbidden. Mom was attached to the idea of rebelling in a secret wedding like *Braveheart* portrayed, telling me that might be my future. But if movies ever had a love scene like that, she had me close my eyes. *That* I was too young for. But I made tiny slits between my fingers to watch the fake sex anyway. There was just... something... about breasts glowing in the moonlight on the eve of revolution.

And then we would go to bed, Mom would sing her songs over me, I would have nightmares related to the movie that I just watched, and then first thing every morning, she would ask me what I had dreamt about.

"I... I saw the sky looked like it was on fire. There was a man with a giant metal sledgehammer that was bashing people's heads in if they didn't follow him, and we escaped in a boat with a few other people down the river. Then I woke up," I said one morning, still shaken up.

She smiled and nodded, saying, "Yes, this is a warning." She told her friends over Bible study. They nodded and kept making preparations, kept updating their timelines of when God was going to start the ball rolling.

Sometimes, when she asked about my dreams, I would lie and say I didn't remember. I didn't want to be God's oracle any more than I wanted the world itself to actually end. I wanted to *see* the world, I wanted to get married and have real sex and have a house with six babies and a golden retriever named Shadow and sunflowers waving in the yard. And *then* maybe Jesus could come back, thank you.

I believed my selfishness must be a stench to God. Here we were, Christians in danger of being put in prison or worse just for speaking the name of the Lord and His mighty deeds—meanwhile, I dared to want Him to hold back His wrath just so I could experience temporary pleasure?

Not my will, but Yours be done. I'm sorry for wanting to be in the world AND of it. Help me live in a way that pleases You and die speaking Your name if necessary. I'll never turn my back on You. Never.

The Road to Canada (1998)

For a while, Mom was convinced the only safe place to ride out Y2K was New Zealand. As an island, it was completely self-sufficient in resources to survive as well as being harder to access for military takeover. I didn't mind the idea of New Zealand; it seemed very far away, but I liked how people talked there, and it looked pretty. Not a bad place to welcome the end.

She changed her mind in the spring of 1998 when we went to our local library to find some books on serious food gardening. An elderly man came up to me, seemingly out of nowhere, and gave me a Canadian one-dollar coin. He called it a loonie. "Don't spend it all in one place," he said with a wink as he walked away.

The loonie had a domino effect on Mom. As soon as she started thinking about Canada and researching Canada, she started seeing clues about Canada everywhere. Seeing the flag or hearing the anthem out in the world when there was absolutely no reason to. Tons of remote real estate was still available, and it would be a lot easier than moving to New Zealand. We were an hour-long drive away from the British Columbia–Montana border and total disappearance.

The following summer, we went on a reconnaissance mission. We drove all through BC, stopping in every town. One night, we attended *Saving Private Ryan* in the theatre, and I couldn't sleep for days.

While Mom kept herself busy in every real estate office she could find, I'd sit in our camper and read the *Left Behind* series. They were stories about the Rapture, when all believers would biblically and mysteriously vanish into thin air, leaving clothes and frightened non-believers behind. Every town that we passed through with no results, Mom said she was just waiting for something that "screamed at her."

Can that something be me? I wondered.

The terrain of BC is multi-faceted. One hour you could be in a rainforest, the next a total desert. We had been driving for hours in the woods of Highway 16 when we rounded a corner, came down a steep hill, and entered the most beautiful valley I'd ever seen. Mountains and rivers and quaint villages reminiscent of Switzerland... this was Smithers.

We found one of the real estate offices on Main Street, and Mom started to get excited when she saw a property listed forty-five minutes out of town. "That's about as remote as you can get!" she said. That same day, a real estate agent took us out to the property. We went up Hudson Bay Mountain, past the ski hill, and onto an old gravel logging road. With every kilometre, I felt a little more dread.

Finally, the thick trees opened up into a marshy field dotted with civilization. It was 314 acres of off-the-grid wilderness, with multiple cabins and barns and a windmill hand-built by a Mennonite family who now had marriageable sons and needed to relocate. The Stocklausers spoke with thick German accents as they gave us a tour and fed us lunch.

As we drove back into town, I looked at Mom's face, and I knew. She had finally heard the screaming, and this was about to be my new home.

The summer that followed was a blur. We spent so many trips going back and forth over the border moving our belongings that I often spent a lot of the travel time reading in the camper above Mom's head.

We made our final move into Canada in September of 1998. I can't say when the date of our last crossing was and I don't remember if I was in the vehicle or in the camper when it happened. All I know is that Mom had papers printed out and stamped for seasonal residents, and that was that.

Glamping

We ran into the woods to hide,
To live "like the Indians did."
We forgot about the fish as we washed
Our hair with Herbal Essences
In their lake.
Did not consider the birds as we burned
Styrofoam plates in the fire because
We were tired of washing dishes.
Never occurred that the trails we mowed
Down on four-wheeled gas guzzlers
Were only there because of four-legged
Grass munchers.
So desperate not to die in the city,
We killed everything in our way.

Stranger in a Strange Land (1998)

Smithers, British Columbia, is one of the most beautiful corners of Canada. Green trees, blue waters, white snowbanks made bearable by the occasional "bluebird day"—the lovely nickname given to days that are cold, but bright and sunny. Smithers is nestled at the base of Hudson Bay Mountain and was noticed by European settlers in the early 1900s because of the planned Grand Trunk Pacific Railway and its requirement of a second major divisional point in BC. The five clans of the Wet'suwet'en people, who still spearfish the Skeena and Bulkley rivers during certain times of the year, lived there first.

That first fall, Mom and I came to town a couple of times a week, and to me it didn't seem like enough time there; it was my favourite. We'd eat at a local restaurant, and then Mom would camp out at the library for the internet, and I was free to roam the streets for hours. The best place to meet kids and hopefully make friends was at the swimming pool or the ice-skating rink. I was desperate to fit in but I had an "accent" and I didn't go to school. I stuck out like a sore thumb. The white kids assumed that I lived on the reserve, and the Native kids inquired which tribe I was from. I didn't know how to engage with any of them. How do you make friends out of strangers when you know that the world is ending soon?

We started living in the two-storey cabin affectionately called Nick's Nest, named after the Mennonite man who'd built every structure to be found on the 314 acres. I wish we'd gotten more of a survival manual from Nick. He and his family had been so self-sufficient, and my mom had once again bought into an idea with no back-up plan.

The first couple of months were naturally an adjustment period, but mentally we had done the work of preparing ourselves already. The oddest thing to get used to was the silence. Out here, there was no traffic, no TV or radio (other than the CB in our truck to keep track of loggers on McDonell Lake Road), no neighbours. Sometimes the wind made the trees crack, or a porcupine scratched its quills against the corner of our barn.

One of the first things Mom taught me about living in the woods was how to keep myself safe and alive in case something happened to her. I learned how to load, fire and clean rifles, and start fires in the pouring rain. I learned what a "lean-to" was (a small shelter made out of sticks), and what a fox sounds like when they bark. Mom always recalls with amusement the day she saw me walk in the fields, suddenly stopping in my tracks. As she watched, I walked again and stopped again. And then I turned and ran as fast as I could toward the house.

"Mom! There was a loud thumping noise in the ground over and over, it sounded like an animal was running toward me!"

She told me through laughter that it was the thumping of a grouse during his mating call.

~

Although I learned from books how to stay alive through many scenarios, I never really needed to employ them, and the only skill that has stood the test of time is my ability to drive stick shift.

We had entered Canada driving a grey Ford F-150 truck from 1988. She was big and long and I had poor depth perception, but Mom stacked books under my butt and put me behind the wheel anyway. She wanted me to imagine that she had slipped and broken her leg or worse, and that my ability to drive the truck quickly and safely for the forty-five-minute drive would be what saved her.

"But Mom, won't the police pull me over for not having a licence?"

"If they pull you over and see the situation, they should escort you to the hospital themselves," she said matter-of-factly.

She made sure I knew where the hospital, the gas station, and third gear were in no time.

We spent a lot of time in town trying to meet people, checking out different churches and going to local events. I spent my eleventh birthday in early October with a couple of girls at the swimming pool, my first time in a hot tub since Jessica had passed, and it was okay. Mom ordered us pizza and gave me a birthday card that said being eleven was like being twice as cool as being number one.

I believed that maybe, in a way, we were getting a fresh start here. New friends who didn't know anything about me before. Maybe I could be a different person too.

Church was a little easier to navigate socially. The congregation on the hill sang the songs we knew, preached the Word, held altar calls. One of the very first evening church services I attended, an assistant pastor and a man named Matt had a scheduled "testimony" time on stage in front of everyone. To everyone's shock, Matt confessed his years-long addiction to pornography, his abusive childhood, his adolescent descent into darkness, his inability to give and receive love as an adult. His shame felt familiar to me.

He said Jesus had finally freed him, and then he demonstrated that by cracking VHS tapes over his knees, black tape billowing like a party streamer. We all applauded him and praised God for this miracle. I harboured a secret curiosity about what was on the tapes.

During another evening service, a young woman named Anna got baptized after testifying that she was done living in rebellion against God and her dad by wanting to wear clothes that were immodest. She was ready to be set apart, even if the world didn't understand; her rebellion and new resolve also felt familiar to me.

It didn't take Mom long to find like-minded people to verbally chew over scriptures and share in her findings from the world wide web. We were often invited to have lunch with various families after the service, and we'd stay the whole afternoon. If there were no kids to play with, there were books to read and family photo albums to explore. I liked to imagine who each stranger in each picture was, and the adventures they'd had. Anything to keep my mind off the Apocalyptic conversation being had in the next room.

Too quickly, the bubble would pop and we'd start making the long drive back up the mountain, and I'd count down the days until we could come back.

And then the snow hit.

Nothing could have prepared us for three feet of snow overnight in the middle of nowhere. Nature didn't care that a mother and daughter were forty-five minutes away from civilization, and the windmill for electric power broke almost immediately. We were stranded for weeks.

We had time, so we filled it. We chopped wood, and tried to make sure the gravity-fed spring water faucet was always turned on a little to prevent freezing. We sliced up the last of our apples to dry on strings across the rafters and practised shooting bullets into empty juice bottles.

If I had any leftover ground beef keeping cold in the snow, I would take it along with a can of stewed tomatoes and a can of kidney beans to make a pot of chili. Real onion if our last one hadn't gone mouldy yet, onion powder if it had.

If the weather was just right on a Sunday, our wind-up radio would catch a broadcast of *Adventures in Odyssey*—a Christian radio program for kids, by Focus on the Family. To this day, the smell of chopped onions sizzling with ground beef still sends me right back to that candle-lit kitchen, and every time the power goes out in my house now, I panic.

We figured out how to navigate a wood-burning stove (and got comfortable with constantly smelling like smoke) and read books on which kind of garden would thrive best here (which would never grow despite our best efforts). We played Phase 10 for hours.

And then one day, after about two weeks at home, a miracle happened: a man named Dave drove his tractor plough through our road like the snow was nothing.

"Hadn't heard from ya on the CB in a while, so I thought I'd just come make sure everything was okay."

He said that farther down the road on McDonell Lake, there was a tourist ranch and old caretaker who lived there during the "off" season, so that was the end of his route. He would try to swing by and make sure our road was clear whenever he could.

I loved Dave. Mom wondered about the ranch and the caretaker, making plans to go visit in the spring.

I found it difficult to even imagine spring. Winter in the wilderness, waiting for the Apocalypse, seemed endless to me.

All Comes Out in the Wash (1999)

Somehow, that winter ended, and while spring brought relief, the beginning of 1999 also introduced a sense of dread: this was the final year before Y2K hit. Our days were a strange mix of ordinary, carrying on as usual, while also preparing for the worst.

We moved out of Nick's Nest into the old original cabin across the field. It was much smaller and would be much easier to keep warm come next winter. I tried not to think about what next winter would be like.

Instead, I focussed on day-to-day life. The cabin itself was in rougher shape, though, and we needed reprieve regularly. It became a habit that once every two weeks, if the roads were drive-able, we would gather all our quarters and all our dirty laundry and make a trip to town. We'd spend a few hours at the laundromat, sharing machines with the tree planters and waiting in line for a real, hot shower. Then we'd fold everything up into a giant pile and take it back out to the truck and would you look at the time! It's almost dinner. So naturally, we'd treat ourselves to a fresh, hot meal anywhere we wanted.

By the time we were finished, it might be dark and dangerous to drive home, so we played it safe and booked a hotel room along the Highway 16 frontage road for the night. For fifty dollars, we could enjoy giant beds, electricity, hot water and cable television for the next sixteen hours.

After months of relying on spring-fed water heated by the fire, sustaining on canned goods, rice and beans and other non-perishable foods (or any nourishment that didn't require refrigeration), working the land trying to grow a garden to no avail, protecting our animals from predators, educating ourselves with books and entertaining ourselves with card games and our imaginations, Laundry Day became my favourite day. A Sabbath, of sorts, for weary wilderness wanderers waiting for a burning bush to speak.

~

Our solitary companion was found in a place called Copper River Ranch. It had owners who were never there, and they hired a caretaker to manage it year-round to host tourists for canoeing, horseback riding, hiking and more. It wasn't long before we met the caretaker, Cowboy, and explored the property and its cabins on McDonnell Lake.

Cowboy was in his seventies and looked like what would happen if the Marlboro Man and a cooked spaghetti noodle made a baby. He had the texture and sound of smoked leather, and he could tell stories while playing cribbage for hours. Sometimes, he liked to show up at our place for a visit, unannounced.

One day, while Mom was taking a nap, I was reading in my room when I heard Cowboy's truck pull up outside. I went into Mom's dark bedroom to let her know he was here, and she sleepily told me to tell him to come back later. Without thinking about how I looked in loose pajama bottoms and its tighter matching tank top, I went outside to say hi.

As usual, he was leaning against the truck with a lit cigarette dangling from his lips. When he saw me, he looked me up and down a couple of times, but we had typical conversation. I told him Mom was napping and prepared for him to leave, but instead he came up behind me, wrapping an arm around my neck and caressing my barely budding breasts with his other hand. I tried to move, but between my shock and his grip, I was frozen. I wished I could float away; hot shame curled in my belly as I heard him make small moaning noises in my ear. Only the trees and their birds were my witnesses.

When he seemed ready to let me leave, I ran back inside without looking back. Mom was putting on her boots to go outside, and asked me if I was okay, but I had one mission: my book, my bed, my room.

I didn't think it had bothered me that much, but a few months later, I attended a week-long summer Bible Camp. One of the nights, our counsellors had us write "letters to God" in which we could say whatever we needed to. Amongst all the other things I might have written to God about—after all, I believed this was the last summer before Y2K came and, with it, the end of the world as I knew it—I wrote about that day with Cowboy. I was under the impression my words would remain anonymous but the following morning my counsellor pulled me aside with the pastors. "You're not in trouble," she said, immediately reading the look on my face. "We just want to ask you about your letter." Shame flooded my cheeks. I was definitely in trouble.

"What you wrote… is that true? Did a man touch you like that?"

I nodded without looking up.

"Have you told anyone except the letter?"

"My mom. She said I didn't have to talk to him again, but he's our only neighbour…."

They seemed relieved. "Okay. But you know that's not your fault, right? You don't have to ask God forgiveness for this. That man should."

It didn't make sense to me. "I wasn't dressed appropriately! I should have been wiser!"

The pastor's wife knelt down in front of me and firmly said, "This is not your fault. We can help you talk to authorities about him if you want, but you should do it anyway. I know it's scary, and you've been very brave. I'm glad you wrote it down."

I couldn't look her in the eye. "I didn't think anyone would read it. I don't need help, I'll figure it out."

They made me make a promise I wasn't sure how to keep.

Later that year, a young girl I knew who would come up to Copper River Ranch to go fishing with her family told me that Cowboy had touched her too and that her family was preparing a case against him. She wanted me to add my testimony, but my mom said no. "But the more people who testify, it could help prove that he did it!" I exclaimed in frustration.

"We can't. It's not our job. God will take care of Cowboy." Mom responded.

I never heard what happened with my friend's case, but not long after, news spread of Cowboy retiring from the Ranch and eventually taking his own life. I never felt bad once. At first, I'd thought that Mom didn't want us to get involved in a court case due to the inevitable interruption of Y2K—and she'd been right: as far as I was concerned, God had taken care of Cowboy for me, and I was grateful.

It would be years before I understood that situations like court cases and testimonies and justice were luxuries that people like me could not afford.

New Year's Eve (1999)

The midsummer and early fall of 1999 brought two things: the dread of the approaching year's end, and new neighbours.

Darryl Davis, his wife, Lisa, and their fifteen-year-old son, Luke, were not only the new caretakers at Copper River Ranch, but they were also Christians preparing for the same fate we were. We felt like we had been given an extraordinary gift; not only did we have friends to survive the end of the world with, but now we had more physical ground to claim for God and storage supplies.

When I first met the Davis family, I was nervous to go back to the Ranch. Cowboy had lived there for decades; surely his presence haunted the grounds. But to my surprise, the dark dusty logs, the cigarette smoke, and the faint smell of alcohol were gone. Lisa's kitchen had been scrubbed and painted white; she played CDs of worship music and collected crushed up eggshells to put in the garden while a tin of coffee percolated on the wood stove. The only remnant of the Cowboy was the cribbage board, and we played countless games. For a time, the Ranch became my refuge.

Mom and Darryl and Lisa would talk and make plans for hours, leaving Luke and me to figure each other out. He was three years older than me, tall with blonde hair and blue eyes, and very quiet. I didn't have a crush on him but I felt like I was supposed to. Who else was meant to be my husband in the godforsaken future, honestly?

On special days, Lisa would teach Luke and me to make homemade bread and stew, and then after dinner, Darryl would fire up the generator long enough to watch a VHS tape of *Shanghai Noon*. When Luke drove me home in the old farm truck, we'd awkwardly clamp our sweaty hands together like two dead fish and hope for feelings to just... appear.

I tried to tell Mom that I wasn't really sure about Luke, but Mom had greater concerns. "Whether you're in love or not, it doesn't change the fact that life in military occupation, especially if I'm gone, will go better for you if you are married. I want you to be safe, babe, love will come later."

But among other things, love never came.

Months passed, and we spent all of them taking 4 x 4 ATVs across the tundra, making storage caches at various landmarks, figuring out which lakes were best for fishing, which sections of "bush" were too thick to cut through, which scriptures were best at laying out a plan for what to expect when the End came. Mom told me to pray for wisdom, and I used my energy to ask God to change His mind at the last minute, like he did for the Ninevites after the prophet Jonah arrived. I had so much I still wanted to do.

Luke increasingly buried himself in his music and writing, occasionally coming up for air to hang out with me. He liked back massages and asked me for them often. I thought it would help him relax, maybe share the innermost workings of his heart. But after a while, I started to feel that old feeling, that feeling of guilt for touching someone else and enjoying it. Sure, Luke was meant to be my husband one day anyway, but this was still flirting too close to the edge. I told him I didn't want to do massages anymore, and he took it personally. I tried to attribute his feelings to the fact that he was sixteen now and that he was also angry at the idea of his future being cut short.

~

December 31, 1999. It was a day which will not live in infamy, except to those of us who thought it would.

Darryl and Lisa hosted a New Year's Eve gathering with a special focus: God's will for the New Year. A friend of theirs named Martin, a prophet, came to spend the evening with all of us, bless our feast, speak over our endeavours, and welcome in the New Year.

The Ranch smelled amazing. Meat had been slow-cooking since the early morning, vegetables preserved from the garden were roasting, yeasty bread was rising high. My eyes widened when I saw multiple bottles of wine in the pantry. Maybe I was finally old enough for a Communion upgrade from grape juice.

The sun had set, and so was the table. Martin invited us to stand for the blessing, speaking a prayer in Hebrew, and then he pulled a gigantic ram's horn out from under his seat.

A shofar. I had heard of them; God's people were called to blow into them at various times throughout history—usually before battle, asking God's Spirit to pour out and declare victory over the enemy.

I didn't know that Martin was not in any way Jewish; I didn't know that it should have mattered.

And no matter who uses it, I do not recommend being in an enclosed space when a shofar is blown.

My ears still ringing, we sat down to dinner. Luke and I sat directly across from each other, but his eyes avoided mine. I started to get annoyed; our lives were about to change forever, and he couldn't even act like my friend?

The wine poured freely, and with it, terrifying conversation. Martin shared about people he'd met around the world, dreamt about, preached to, prophesied over. Demons being cast out, angels disguised as hitchhikers, Christians in danger and being physically transported to a different part of the country for safety, through the God portal.

And if we thought people deceived by the Devil were all we had to worry about, it was time to watch the skies. Martin explained there was an underground facility in Alaska called HAARP (High-frequency Active Auroral Research Program) that was changing the weather but being covered up and sold as "global warming"; and those contrails that lingered in the sky long after the jets had flown over were actually "chemtrails"—streams of toxins coating the lungs of healthy citizens so they'd be vulnerable to any sickness the government decided to release.

Across the sea, Russia and China were preparing for war and had been secretly transporting guillotines and tanks on our Cosco train cars for years; America, the whore of Babylon, wasn't ready.

Mom hung onto every word like Martin was Christ Himself.

As the hours passed and scriptures from Daniel and Revelation were pored over and the wine poured out, I felt like I wanted to vomit. After years of being prepared (desensitized, Mom called it), I was quickly losing tolerance for people who seemed to be excited at the thought of millions being lost to war and famine and disease.

Finally, feeling like something other than myself was possessing my body, I grabbed the nearest bottle of wine, drank a huge gulp, and yelled,

"Will EVERYONE please stop talking about this! I am ABSOLUTELY SICK of it!" I slammed the bottle back on the table.

The atmosphere changed very quickly. The adults were gasping, Luke was smirking, chairs were scraping across the floor frantically.

Mom said, "I think it's time to go home," with a tinge of embarrassment and I felt ashamed. I knew everyone expected an apology, but I was still too angry. Stomping out in the snow brought cool relief to my heated cheeks.

Mom and I drove the ten snowy kilometres home and went to bed wordlessly. I couldn't sleep while I waited for midnight—for the end to begin.

Part Two

January 1, 2000

The dry wood cracked as fresh flames licked its edges, loud enough to shake me out of an empty dream. My eyes took a minute to adjust to the bright morning light, my body confused by the way I was lying and what I was covered in.

Oh, right. I wasn't in my closet-room. I had taken a sleeping bag out to the living room and slept on the couch last night. I'd made myself stay up until midnight, staring out the living room window at the jagged backside of Hudson Bay Mountain. I'd seen the very slight tinge of orange outlining the peaks as the New Year's Eve night glowed from town.

I'd been waiting. For what, I wasn't sure. A giant cosmic light? A booming sound? Anything different to indicate that the clock had struck midnight and Y2K was indeed here.

But I'd seen nothing. Maybe I fell asleep and missed it? Surely, that must be it.

The rest of my senses came to life in an instant when I heard the camping kettle start bubbling, sending wafts of fresh coffee steam in my direction. I didn't actually like the taste of coffee, but I'd wear it as perfume if I could.

The realization hit me. Mom was awake. She'd started a fire and made coffee. Maybe she knew more about what happened last night.

What happened last night is that you lost it on everyone, and Mom had to bring you home, remember?

I rolled over in the sleeping bag, my face wrinkling into a chagrined expression. I sat up, preparing myself for a lecture, but she was just sitting in front of the fire, poking it occasionally with a long piece of metal. I looked out the window; it was a clear day and the animals were already eating contentedly. Everything looked exactly as it had for the past two years.

"Morning, babe." Her calm voice broke the silence. "How did you sleep?"

I got up and walked over to warm my hands in front of the fire and smell the coffee closer. "Not bad. What time is it?"

"After ten. You were tired. I couldn't sleep, too much to think about today."

Drip. Drip. Drip. I could hear the water coming out of the faucet ever so slightly and I sighed with gratitude. The spring had been running all night, and we'd have water today. I wanted oatmeal for breakfast.

But first. "Did anything happen at midnight? I stayed out here to see, but I must have fallen asleep."

Mom got up to rinse a mug in the sink and pour herself a cup of coffee. "I don't think so. The roads weren't bad coming home last night, though, so I was thinking maybe we could drive to the ski hill entrance, put on the radio and see if there's anything on the news."

That made sense to me. Close enough to town, but not too close, just in case folks were already rioting in the streets.

As we made breakfast, I felt like we were playing Chicken about the night before. Who was going to bring up my outburst first? Was I going to apologize—did I even want to?

Finally, I couldn't take it anymore, and I said, "Are you mad about my behaviour last night?"

She paused in eating her oatmeal and looked at me for a moment, almost with a gaze of sadness. "No. We adults get pretty caught up in everything sometimes, and you're already so mature for your age, I forget that you're still a kid."

I stirred my oatmeal, not able to do anything except stare at the gluey grains.

"The next time we see the Davis family, you can say you're sorry, though. They really did make such a nice evening for us."

I nodded. Right now, I didn't really ever want to see the Davis family again, but what choice did I have?

~

Within an hour, we were bundled up and ready to drive the twenty-odd kilometres to the ski hill. Mom let me drive, as she knew I needed more practice in snowy conditions. I loved driving, but I couldn't fight the dread that filled my arms and legs the closer I brought us to our new reality.

The first day of the new year was half over by the time we parked in the gravel quarry next to the ski hill turn-off. I took a deep breath, we looked at each other, and I turned the radio on.

"... this is your twelve o'clock news...first of all, congratulations to the first babies of the New Year born in BC today! This is perhaps the most unique birth announcement we've had in a while. The Miller family in Vancouver welcomed a baby last night at 11:58 p.m., December thirty-first, 1999...and then moments later, a second baby was born on January first, 2000! So not only were these twins born on different days and different years... but different millenniums."

This was today's top news? I mean, it was extremely neat, but... what?

Mom and I decided to go into town, so we switched seats. Even if I'd been old enough to drive within city limits, my head was so full of confused thoughts, I would not have been able to focus.

Smithers did look a little different since the last time we saw it. All of the Christmas decorations were gone, and the streets were quiet. But it was New Year's Day and just about everything was closed, just like it was any other year. People were staying warm in their homes, soaking up what remained of their days off with family. We drove through neighbourhoods still lit up with electricity and TVs and computers. Cars new enough to have computer chips in them were roaming freely. Kids were playing, dogs were barking, cats were snoozing.

The world was still here.

Now Mom and I were playing Chicken again. Who was going to break the awkward silence and state the obvious?

This time, she beat me. "The date must have been wrong. It's still going to happen this year, it's just... going to happen slower than we expected. That must be it."

There's a verse in the New Testament where Jesus says even if you have faith as small as a mustard seed, it is enough to plant and grow an entire tree of belief.

I wondered if the same could be said for a seed of doubt.

My Body Is a Stranger (2000)

As the new millennium settled into her paces without a hiccup, the foundation in the wall of my belief began to crumble. Which is odd considering that I *had* asked God to change His mind and let us, let the world, live.

Mom noticed I was losing interest in my Bible homework almost right away. It wasn't like I didn't believe in it anymore, it was just that my sense of urgency had been removed. I was starting to swallow pieces of the Bread of Life with a few grains of salt, questioning whether a verse was literal or allegorical. Mom said it was good to question things, of course, but the greatest trick the Devil could pull on us now was to make us think nothing was going to happen after all.

But our weekly trips to town continued to happen uninhibited, Dave the ploughman and weather willing.

We had almost survived our second winter when our ordinary little unordinary life took an unexpected turn. Living off-the-grid was a feat of constant physical activity. Even though we were fortunate enough to have a gravity-fed spring with running water, every day we were chopping and stacking cords of wood, trying to estimate how much we'd need to get through the winter. Lifting hay bales for animals that acted like we were starving them. Cutting brush and gutting fish and shovelling paths through the snow to get from the house to the barn and back. Moving storage supplies around from barn to barn. I had already started wearing glasses and my hands were scarred with burns and cuts from relying on oil lamp light or candles.

By the time February rolled around, Mom told me that she hadn't been feeling well for a while. We were sitting at the dining room table sharing a pot of my homemade chili when she told me that she had been pushing it off for as long as she could, but she needed to see a doctor.

"When I was pregnant with you, I developed a benign fibroid tumour on my uterus. Doctors removed it at the time, but the way I've been feeling lately... I think it's returned."

I didn't know what to think, then. I still don't know what to think now. I have no idea how she afforded herself a full hysterectomy in a Canadian hospital out of pocket, but she did, over a weekend in February. I stayed with a family from church and prayed at the altar that Sunday morning for her. I wasn't even thirteen and contemplating what I would need to do if she inexplicably orphaned me.

Once again, my fears were unfounded, and Mom recovered well. She knew the best way to heal was to keep moving, so that's exactly what she did. She was relieved to be done with the pain, with menstruation, with the possibility of a tumour ever returning. Surviving the end of the world would be so much easier without a pesky uterus.

~

Mom's decades of menstruation might have come to an end, but mine were just beginning.

I knew what a period was, and what it accomplished and why. But it still took me by surprise. I already had a bad habit of holding my bladder first thing in the morning in favour of sleep, but on that spring morning, I woke up feeling like I had waited too long and I panicked. I threw off my covers and ran to the bathroom so dramatically that it made Mom call out, "Are you okay?"

"NO!" I shrieked, staring at the bright shock of red in my underwear and pajama pants. My stomach churned like I had food poisoning, and my chest ached. Surely, I would never be okay ever again.

I heard Mom's voice outside the door. "Did you get your period?"

Tears inexplicably filled my eyes. "How did you know?"

A muffled chuckle. "A mama knows."

"I can't even move off the toilet right now," I sobbed. "Why is God doing this to me? What purpose could this *possibly* serve?"

"You're a woman now," Mom said. "It's going to be okay. Can I help you?"

I didn't feel like a woman. I felt like a disaster.

Lord, I take it all back. I don't want to grow up or get married or have babies. All I want is to never feel like this again. Take me now, please.

"No one can help me," I said despondently. This development felt like pouring salt in the wound of already too many responsibilities. What was the point of being able to create life when my future held only death?

The bathroom door opened, and Mom was standing there with a fresh set of clothes for me. "I'm gonna teach you some tricks to get through this, okay babe? I couldn't even get out of bed to go to school when I first got my period, so I understand. Give me your clothes."

She proceeded to show me how to rinse the blood out well enough to keep it from setting before we could get to the laundromat in town. She got me Tylenol and started heating water for a hot water bottle. I was starting to feel a little more in control, and then she showed me the Tampax.

I gave it my best effort, I really did. But there was absolutely no way that a foreign object was going inside of my body. It was tight and it hurt and there were way too many places for that long cotton ball on a string to get lost. I was closed for business.

Great. Now I'm able to make babies, and I can't even handle the logistics of what makes the babies!

Mom gave me a giant winged maxi-pad, telling me not to worry, that I could try Tampax again later. This was why she had purchased a lot of both products.

She left so I could clean myself up and change my clothes. The pad made me feel like I was waddling; surely anyone who saw me in town would know that I was bleeding out whenever I was wearing one! Would the injustices never end?

I was finally ready to leave the bathroom and all I wanted to do was crawl back into bed and go to sleep. I saw even more blood on my sheets and started crying again.

How many laundromat quarters was I going to need from now on? What was I going to do when the laundromat was no longer an option?

~

Summer was by far my favourite season in Apocalypse Land. The smells of melting winter and spring mud gave way to green grass and alpine flowers, and freedom still felt like a possibility. I was constantly torn between the "what if" of when our lives would change forever, and seizing every available moment of normalcy I had left.

Luke Davis had turned seventeen and gone in the complete opposite direction. We never talked about that New Year's Eve night; in fact, he never really talked to anyone. He just decided he wasn't going to be a part of whatever we were up to anymore, and he got himself a job as a line cook in Hudson Bay Mountain's main lodge. He became roommates with some other cooks who were living in a house along Railway, his parents leaving Copper River Ranch to go visit him every couple of weeks. I think they were worried.

Mom was okay with me doing occasional extracurricular activities away from the wilderness, as long as they still served a purpose. When I found an ad in the local newspaper for a weekend-long horse camp at the Northern Lights Wildlife Society, Mom thought it sounded like a great idea.

I had ridden horses a few times when we still lived in Montana, but someone else had always been responsible for their saddling and care. This camp gave a crash course in everything important about horses, and being able to fully saddle, ride the trails, and safely put everything away when you were done was like the exam at the very end. Trying to remember every step-by-step instruction was challenging for my brain, but thankfully I connected with another girl there who was already about to get her first horse at home.

Her name was Kass, and she was my age, maybe a little bit younger. She was tall and angular with long dark hair and big dark eyes. I had actually seen her at church and the swimming pool a few times before, but she seemed shy and I hadn't wanted to bother her. Now we and our horses were partnered together for the whole weekend. By the end of it, I smiled, feeling hope in my heart that not only had I learned a new skill, but made a friend.

Kass's mom and my mom met when they came to pick us up. Kass's mom was so thrilled we had connected that she gave us her phone number right away. We didn't know how to explain our phoneless situation quite yet, so we simply said, "We'll call you."

Kass and her little brothers became a constant in my life. We spent the whole summer playing outside at their house, going to Tyhee Lake and watching movies when it got dark and Mom said I could stay the night if Kass's mom said it was okay. It was always okay.

Occasionally they liked to watch movies that I wasn't sure I was allowed to, with themes of magic and fantasy, but I just snuggled up in my sleeping bag and pretended to fall asleep until it was over, or until I actually did fall asleep.

By the time the summer was coming to a close, we had explained a little more in-depth about where we lived to Kass's parents, and they said it was okay for Kass to come stay the weekend with me. Opening up my strange world to someone who had only ever gone camping for fun felt like an exercise in trust. Would she have fun? Would she see the guns and the piles of books and the dried apple slices on strings across the kitchen ceiling that we never ate, and never come back?

But I needn't have worried. Mom had promised me she wouldn't talk about any Apocalypse stuff, and she kept it. We played in the creek for hours and roasted marshmallows on the campfire. We rode horses and went fishing in canoes at Copper River Ranch.

For the first time in years, I almost felt... normal. Before long, I craved it.

~

My town life slowed down once school arrived in September again. I tried to start my grade seven textbooks, but there were so many winter preparations to be made. I opened my science book to the first page, which was "How A Light Bulb Works," and I immediately closed it. As far as my brain was concerned, electricity was akin to magic. I could read well and write well and do basic math decently. I did not understand how science worked, least of all electricity, and I was part of a world that didn't need to. Mom and I still used oil lamps and candles.

What we did need was firewood, as always, and we were expanding our farm supplies to make our third winter a little easier. We bought two Polaris snowmobiles so we could still travel independently even if Dave didn't show up, and two white geese to try and deter the fox activity in our chicken coop. They were hissy and ornery, and the back of my leg developed occasional bruises from them using their beaks as weapons. Surely, the foxes stood no chance.

We brought the geese home right away to get adjusted to their new environment, and the snowmobiles stayed in the barn, waiting for the first snowfall.

We didn't have to wait long. Every decade or so in Smithers there would be one giant snowfall when the snow would fall an entire day and night before Halloween. This was that year. Kids were suddenly challenged with fitting their costumes overtop of their snow gear and parents walked the streets with them, carrying hot chocolate. The early snow didn't impact any Halloween celebrations for us, of course, but an early snow meant another long winter, even longer than before.

Thanks to the snowmobiles, however, the winter was a lot more fun than it had been before. Learning how to use them was very different from the four-wheel ATVs we were accustomed to. Those four wheels relied on solid ground, but with skis and a track I felt like I was floating across the glistening fields and lakes. I could shift my weight ever so slightly and go in a completely different direction.

Humming like an angry bee, I could make constellations in the snow with my tracks. I hung onto tidbits of information like the following: as long as I drove at least forty miles per hour, I could skim across any wet spots; my armpit was the warmest part of my body and I could tuck my hands in if they got cold; if I tipped over, push it back upright immediately or the engine will flood. And most importantly: Don't drive farther than I'm willing to walk home.

~

The winter passed, and our chickens survived. Whether the geese had done their job or the foxes had moved on, we were extremely pleased with ourselves. Maybe any other pioneer would have laid awake at night with a gun for those foxes, but ours were basically wall decoration at this point, as we were trying to conserve ammunition. We had prepared for the isolation to bring us all manner of wilderness creatures: moose, bobcat, bear. But we didn't see anything, and we got used to that. Maybe the previous decades of logging had already made our land feel inhospitable to anything larger than a grouse.

So one morning in March of 2001, I went out onto the front porch to gather chopped wood like I always did, not even registering the large brown shape that was rustling the brush on the other side of the fence, perhaps fifteen feet away from me.

The grizzly bear let out a small warning roar and I jumped, dropping the wood; I think he was just as surprised to see me as I was to see him. I froze on the porch, adrenaline sending spikes of dread through my limbs. I couldn't remember what to do with grizzly bears—do I make myself big and threatening or small and not worth bothering? Do I run back inside? Surely, the house could withstand a bear attack.

We just stared at each other for a moment. Hibernation was probably ending and he was hungry. *You can take a goat or a sheep if you want*, I tried to tell him. *Just please let me leave. My gun is all the way up in the barn, and I can barely aim, trust me. Carry on, friend.*

Suddenly, I heard muffled yelling, and I slowly turned around to see my mom standing on the other side of the kitchen window with a wide-eyed panic on her face. "A bear! A bear! A bear!" she shrieked, pointing. Annoyed, I forgot myself and yelled back, "I know! I know! I know!" Then I grabbed two pieces of wood and by sheer force of will made my legs put me back inside the house. Mom shakily locked the door behind me.

For the next hour or so, we watched this magnificent animal rumble through the brush to find berries while absolutely ignoring us in the cabin, and our sheep and goats in their easily accessible pen.

Maybe he'd heard my thoughts. Maybe he'd been annoyed by our dramatics. Maybe he was simply a bear, waking up to another year like he always had, discovering there were still other signs of life here.

Our guns never left the barn walls.

~

Now that I was officially a teenager, Mom decided to keep her promise to our Montana dentist and took us in for the first cleaning and checkup we'd had in over three years.

Thankfully, our sealants had held up pretty well, and cavities were practically non-existent, but Dr. Kinkela—a widely respected dentist in the Bulkley Valley for many years—came to the same conclusion: I needed braces, badly.

Mom was still concerned about me being trapped with metal-mouth at the end of the world, but by now, claiming it as financially beyond us was also a little more true. I couldn't even calculate how much we'd spent on Apocalypse supplies, most of which were still waiting to be used.

Mom asked Dr. Kinkela if there were any alternatives. He hesitated, and then offered, "We could pull one of her front teeth on the side where it's not as noticeable, and then her teeth would naturally shift and have a little more room. I don't recommend it, but it's a lot more financially accessible."

Mom grinned. "That sounds great, let's do that."

His brow furrowed. "I need you to understand that, if we do this, getting braces in the future won't be a good idea. Because her teeth will shift again, so she'll be left with a gaping hole and need an implant. I don't like pulling teeth for no reason."

Mom held up her hand like a scout. "I promise we won't be getting braces anytime in the future. Let's take care of this now."

They barely took a minute to include me in the conversation, and before I knew it, I was lying under another bright light and wincing at the needle going into my gums to numb the area. By this time, I had seen *Castaway* in the movie theatre because Mom thought it seemed like "our kind of story," and I was just grateful I wasn't deserted on an island with only an ice skate and a coconut to knock out my tooth like Tom Hanks.

Recovery was unpleasant. The empty gap and the taste of blood left me feeling on edge. Dr. Kinkela assured me that even though it would be slow, my teeth would move and it would be like the gap was never there.

It seemed like I was always being reassured that everything changing in and about my body was something I had to get used to. My feelings and choices didn't really matter as long as the greater good was accomplished, and that had made more sense when I was younger. But now? I was starting to wish the greater good actually felt good too.

9/11 (2001)

Not only did the year 2000 pass by with nary a blip on the Apocalypse radar, so did 2001… almost.

In addition to the reading of novels, writing of book reports, and Bible study I did sporadically and with little enthusiasm at home in our cabin, in the late summer of 2001, I signed up for piano and voice (solo and quartet) lessons once a week with a woman from our church named Sharon. Music and music theory was still important to my mom, and she'd been impressed by Sharon's frequent worship accompaniments on Sunday mornings.

The arrangement was perfect: I had all my lessons back to back on Tuesday, then I and the three other quartet girls—one of whom was Kass—would make dinner with Sharon's youngest teenage daughter, Vee, and then we'd all catch a ride with her to the youth group at our church on the hill.

I didn't understand why, with the Apocalypse surely about to happen any moment now, my mother was prioritizing music lessons—surely butchering animals was a more practical life skill for the end of the world—but I didn't question it. Attending music lessons, and with other girls, too, was the closest thing to normalcy I had experienced since we moved from Montana to Smithers, aside from my horse-riding with Kass, and I wanted more of it.

Learning piano proved tricky without an instrument to practise on at home; I also found the dyspraxic coordination I'd experienced in early grade school returning, but in my hands. I'd thought I was just a clumsy kid who'd grow out of it, but now, since I didn't know what was actually causing it, I wondered if I was just not good at doing things. Watching sheet music with my eyes and focussing on making my hands do two different things at the same time made me feel dizzy. Those lessons lasted less than a semester.

Singing and hearing harmonies, however? That came as naturally as breathing. Our quartet was called TLC—Teens Loving Christ—and we took great pleasure in learning the latest pop songs in Christian Contemporary Music, and then performing them during the church offering once a month. Mom wasn't as interested in going to church anymore, as repentance from sin was not preached enough, but she showed up every time I sang. I began to feel like there were two different Carlys that existed: the pure, joyful Christian who believed in the goodness of God and loved reading the Word, singing His Praise—and the scared, lonely, mad prophet who was about to be thrown into the lion's den.

~

Mom liked to make a day of our music trips, so we'd head out in the truck early on Tuesday mornings. We would listen to worship CDs and my voice lesson tape recorder to keep me warmed up for the day, and then there was always a certain point on the forty-five-minute logging road journey when the radio would come back on.

One Tuesday in September, I heard a song I'd never heard before, and I'll never forget it. Something about this man's voice, the instrumentation, the words left me deeply unsettled. What was coming in the air tonight?

Once the song ended, the top-of-the-hour news crackled to life: "A candlelight vigil will be held tonight for those who lost their lives in the New York City tragedy this morning...."

Mom turned up the radio. "What did they say happened?"

I shrugged and shook my head, feeling that familiar pit in my stomach.

Once we got to town, we stopped for breakfast at our regular Main Street coffee shop, Kokopelli Café. It only took asking one person to find out about the planes that flew into the World Trade Center hours earlier. The pit in my stomach became jelly in my legs and I had to sit down.

I remembered the song I'd heard on the radio; yes, I'd been waiting for this moment my whole life, oh Lord. A prayer that sounded like a threat.

This was it. The beginning of the end of America, the world.

Mom immediately went to the library to use a computer; I knew that's where she'd be for the rest of the day. I was able to keep myself together long enough to walk to Sharon's house that afternoon, and the TLC quartet watched the New York footage over dinner. It felt surreal for our life here to be continuing as usual; how could I explain to these friends that everything had changed? In my mind, I prepared for this to be the last time I saw any of them.

~

Mom would never admit it, but I think the failure of Y2K had shaken her faith just like mine. The event of September 11 seemed to reignite her spark, and we started going into town way more so that her research could continue.

The realtor who had sold us the cabin was no longer a realtor and had bought the local Subway restaurant on the corner of Highway 16 and Main Street. He had an office in the back with a good internet connection, and since he hated doing office work even more than he had hated being a realtor, he let Mom use it nearly anytime she wanted.

I had always loved the smell of warm bread that permeated my nostrils every time I entered a Subway, but I spent so many hours there over the next year that I hardly noticed it anymore. Mom would have preferred that I did some kind of schoolwork, but she didn't enforce it, so I spent time reading, washing dishes and running tomatoes or cucumbers through an industrial grade slicer that I was not qualified to use.

When I got tired of being there, I would walk all over town. It didn't take long, and I don't know what I was looking for, but I would go up and down Main Street three or four times in a row, looking in the shop windows, glancing at the parking lots. Did I see anyone I knew, or any of their vehicles that indicated they might be nearby? Maybe if I hung around the drugstore or the bookstore long enough, a friend would come along.

Sometimes I went the other direction and followed groups of kids walking to or from the high school. If I planned it right, I could have my bathing suit and towel already with me and follow people I didn't know into the nearby pool. Even if I had no one to swim with, I enjoyed admiring everyone else in their bright colours and shimmering skin. I wondered how it would feel to look like *that*.

On Main Street days, I'd sit in Kokopelli Café and buy an Italian soda so that I could read magazines and people-watch. I loved browsing Northern Drugs for Archie Comics and trying on makeup samples. I'd crouch down and hide in between the bookshelves of SpeeDee Interior Stationery bookstore to read. If I was in a more spiritual mood, I'd walk to the Bible bookstore just around the corner from SpeeDee to read or listen to demo music there, ignoring Mom's voice in my head that said reading books without paying was rude.

Doing this kept me involved in the hustle and bustle of town while still going mostly unnoticed. I learned which teenagers were dating who and overheard my piano teacher, Sharon, announce to the entire store that her first grandchild, a girl named Delaney Frances Elliott, had been born to her daughter, Michelle, and son-in-law, Calvin.

I longed to accidentally bump into someone else's plans and be invited to join in. I must have looked so odd—me with my off-balance gait and my heart longing to be called "sister."

~

By October of 2001, we had been living on our property forty-five minutes from Smithers for three years. I had just turned fourteen and, even though I was starting to make more friends through the church youth group, I still felt like I was acting in a role. I could only fully be myself with people who were on the same page as we were, and those were few and far between. I caught myself mentioning theories about the government and their inevitable takeover, or whether the Rapture was going to happen pre/mid/post Tribulation, and all I got in return were stares and awkward jokes about my being American.

"You don't even look American, what are you?" the youth group boys teased.

I swallowed with difficulty. "Well, my mom says my grandma on my dad's side was from Mexico...."

The youth group girls came over and joined in, wanting to impress the boys. They all looked at each other and laughed. "Oh, you're a Mexican! No wonder you're a border-crosser scared of the government! Ay ay ay!" They all cheered in fake Spanish accents.

I was nicknamed the Crazy Mexican after that. I never quite understood why, or what was funny about it. I wished that I didn't look a certain way that seemed to prompt people to ask "what" I was. I had never seen anyone else that looked like me before; my dad could have been an alien from outer space for all I knew. I kept telling myself they were just joking, that this was part of friendship, that it meant I belonged.

Kass was starting to grow out of her shyness and become more popular, so she introduced me to a few kids who were a bit nicer. If I happened to be in town at the same time as their lunch hour from school, they said I could come over to their cafeteria and hang out; it gave me something to look forward to.

I wanted things to look forward to. I wanted a *life* to look forward to. One of my favourite verses had always been Jeremiah 29:11, about the Lord having plans to give me hope and a future. But ever since the Twin Towers had fallen and my mom had started her research again in renewed urgency, I didn't know what future there was to look forward to. Without a framework for hope or joy even in the midst of suffering, my future felt like a candlelit room with no door. Whatever life held, it looked like my peers were going to be finding out without me.

~

While other teenagers were busy with high school and sports and family dinners, I was still navigating a life that mostly revolved around my mother, her beliefs, and her whims. Even though Mom hadn't entirely run out of the inheritance-money-traded-for-gold-and-silver yet, she tried to employ quick ways to make some extra cash. This included adopting two springer spaniels named Blue and Olivia and having them procreate—a lot.

I was in my element, helping Olivia deliver her puppies, and Kass loved to come out for weekend sleepovers to get some puppy love.

One litter "came of age" in the winter of 2001, but getting them to town to be sold was complicated. Mom and I each had a backpack, and we would carefully put the puppies inside, get our snow gear on, fire up the snowmobiles and ride twenty kilometres to the ski hill.

Once there, the road became ploughed again, so we would hide the rigs in the trees, and start walking down the mountain into town. If we got lucky, someone heading down would pick us up and drop us off at the Safeway; from there, we would set up a puppy camp. All day long, I would stand at one automatic door, and Mom would stand at the other, holding beautiful brown-and-white or black-and-white springer spaniel puppies, hoping that shoppers would be ready to drop three hundred dollars' cash the minute they saw us.

Miraculously, we did sell a few puppies, but it was slow work, spread over a few weekends. Before it got dark, we would do our shopping inside, transfer puppies and groceries into backpacks, and then start hitchhiking back up the ski hill road. It was not as common to get picked up then, unfortunately.

One weekend, I was feeling under the weather, so Mom took the puppies in one backpack and went to town by herself. I was in charge of feeding the animals and keeping the fire going all day. I made supper and anticipated the distant hum of the snowmobile to sound at any moment.

I lit candles and read books, trying to think of reasons why Mom wasn't home yet. At least, now that it was dark, I would see the headlight of her arrival coming from a kilometre away.

I startled awake, checking the time: 1:00 a.m. The fire was almost out, and I hastily put more wood on, checking Mom's room. Surely, I would see her blanketed form lying peacefully asleep.

Nothing.

Fear became a living thing crawling up my throat. My heart was pounding and I started praying out loud. "In the name of Jesus, protect her, guide her, transport her home! Do not take her from me yet! I promise I will read your Word and pray and listen so much more, just please bring her home in Jesus's name!"

For an hour, I paced and prayed and planned. If morning came and she wasn't here, I could fire up the other snowmobile and go to Copper River Ranch to ask Darryl and Lisa Davis for help. This is what I had trained for, after all.

Suddenly, I heard a loud thump on the porch. A dark shadow was coming to the door, and once again I wished a gun was closer by. I thought about grabbing the metal fire poker, but before I could, the door opened, and I saw Mom's cherry-red face peeking out from a layer of fur and snow.

"I'm home!" she said breathlessly, putting the backpack on the floor. "We're all alive. At least, I think so."

The puppies.

Mom began to slowly shed her layers while I opened the backpack. Thankfully, there they were all nestled, warm and asleep. "I made it to

Hankin Lake Road, four kilometres out," Mom said. "But that fresh snow covered up an icy rut, and we tipped over; the snowmobile flooded and wouldn't start again no matter how long I waited. So I started walking."

The water I'd put on the stove was warm and ready for Mom's bath. I poured it as she continued.

"Thank goodness I packed the snowshoes, but the snow was so wet and heavy on top of them, I must have been lifting an extra ten pounds on each foot. I got to the point where I had to decide, I can't carry both backpacks anymore, I'm gonna have to leave the groceries or the puppies. And I wasn't willing to lose these puppies."

I left her as she got into the bath, groaning. I checked the time; almost three in the morning. The sheep, goats, chickens and geese would be up in a few hours, so I tried to go back to bed. It took a while for the fear to crawl back down my throat into my stomach, where it belonged, and I watched the sun come up.

Mom slept for twelve hours after that bath. I went outside and fed all the mewling creatures, coming back inside to check on her. Still breathing. I chopped wood and tended the fire and melted snow and cuddled the puppies. When Mom finally emerged, she was starving and ready to go find the groceries. We took the second snowmobile across the field, only going about two kilometres before we saw the backpack peeking out of the snow.

Our usual "snow fridge" had acted more like a freezer; the only casualty of that long night was a bag of navel oranges, which turned to mush as soon as they thawed out on the kitchen table.

Relocation (2002–2003)

Even though I had lived behind a ski hill for three years now, I had never actually gone skiing. I figured with my history of clumsiness it was neither attainable nor smart. But now it was a regular occurrence for my friends to spend the whole day up on the hill, and they offered to teach me how. I didn't have my own gear, obviously, so Mom gave me enough money to rent some for the day and grab some lunch while I was there. I spent all morning successfully on the bunny hill with Kass and my new friend Elijah Marshall. His mom worked at the Bible Bookstore and had befriended the odd girl who liked to read books and listen to the current demo CDs (she even let me take old ones home that were no longer in rotation, so with the help of my Discman, I learned thirty-second segments of Christian Contemporary Music by heart).

Mrs. Marshall had sent Elijah up the hill with enough snacks to feed an army, so Kass and I got in line to buy some poutine for lunch. Suddenly a familiar face in the kitchen caught my eye.

Luke Davis.

I hadn't seen him in months; I almost didn't recognize him. He'd grown his hair and beard long, and he had an earring now. He must have felt me staring, because he looked up right at me, and then did a quick head nod like a nonverbal *hey*.

I nodded *hey* back.

Kass, never missing much, caught our silent interaction. "Carly, do you know that guy?"

How did I explain this? "Kind of," I said, picking up my tray and heading back to the table.

"He's cute! And so much older, I'm impressed!"

I blushed, hoping this attention would end by the time we got back to the table and Elijah. I kind of liked *him*. And there was no way I was going to delve into my weird connection to Luke.

I needn't have worried. Elijah was focussed on which trail he was going to graduate me to now that I had conquered the bunny hill. I had fallen a lot, but he was extremely patient and believed that I was ready.

"I know advanced math is your thing, but you have absolutely overestimated the physics I am capable of here," I told him.

"Nah, you'll be fine," he replied, his toque-messed brown hair and blue eyes twinkling in a way that made my stomach flip. I would try anything if Elijah believed in me.

Four hours later, Mrs. Marshall picked up three exhausted teenagers and took them back to her family room for hot chocolate, frozen pizza and movies. It was perfect.

Days like this always ended too quickly, but I treasured them deeply, taking mental photographs that I hoped I'd be able to access in my mind once everything had come to an end.

~

Instead of thinking about driver's licences, first jobs, and college applications like my friends were starting to do, I was busy listening to my mother making alternate arrangements for the Apocalypse that she was still sure was going to come any day now. It hadn't come on the very first day of the millennium, but surely the attack on New York City was a sign of things to come.

And so, we continued to wait, and while we waited, perhaps, my mom thought, we should be more comfortable. On one end of McDonell Lake lay Copper River Ranch with which, by now, we were well acquainted. We knew of a few other fishing and hunting cabins in the surrounding areas and had made storage caches near them for future getaways, but our excitement grew when we heard that a large property with a massive hunting cabin at the other end of McDonell Lake was up for sale. In the spring of 2002, Mom bought it and then continued doing what she had done best for years: hire a team of contractors to build a brand new house, by her design. I cannot even begin to imagine the cost of a two-hour daily commute plus transporting supplies through a poorly made hunting path in the woods. But as the house started to take shape, I started to imagine my room, with butterfly wallpaper. Imagine a home with a lakefront view, with solar panel electricity. A fresh start.

While it was being built, Mom debated selling our current home; we were beginning to feel the pinches of spending. Maybe we should abandon this section of the woods altogether and fortify our resources at the lake for good.

~

Sometimes, when we really wanted a break from the wilderness life, Mom would swear me to secrecy and we'd take a four-hour trip to the city of Prince George. We'd stay in a nice hotel, eat anything we wanted, and browse at the local pawn shop to trade gold, silver and antiques for cash. And then on the way home, we'd stop at Costco and fill the truck with bags of rice and beans, canned goods, sanitary pads, garden seeds, clothes twice my size that I could grow into. Deep down, I thought I'd never live long enough to wear them.

We spent back-breaking hours carting sealed garbage bins of food and supplies on a floating barge across the lake. Sometimes, on the other weekends, my friends would come out to help, and Mom would pay them too. "A labourer is worthy of his hire," she would often quote.

And then as the sun went down, she would take us all into town and treat us to dinner at the pizzeria. If her people asked questions, I never knew.

As an experiment, Mom put our home up for sale in the summer of 2002, just to "see if anyone would bite." She listed it for higher than we'd purchased it, as we'd built so many extra storage structures. Two weeks later, we went on a road trip to Kamloops to visit a family from our Smithers church who had moved there a couple of years back. We stayed with them for a week, and Mom didn't get any emails from our realtor during this time.

When we drove back to Smithers, we checked in with the realtor's office. No bites. Mom was a bit discouraged; she was hoping to have everything settled before another winter came. "It's such a unique property, it'll just have to be for the right person," she reassured herself.

We made it back home in the early evening, only to see a note taped to our door. We looked at each other with curiosity; this form of communication had never happened before. Mom opened it and her smile got really big. The note said, "Hi, we are two campers visiting BC from the US, and we absolutely LOVE your property! Can we talk about buying it? We are camped up the hill off the main trail, and we hope you get this message in time."

The note was dated from two days previous.

We were buzzing with excitement as we hopped back in the truck and went in search of the campers. It didn't take long. They were up on the hillside as they'd said, and when they saw us, they got up from around the campfire and started waving excitedly. This man and his girlfriend had been looking for a way to leave the US and live off-the-grid, and less than a week later, a deal was struck.

Ben and Charissa were very excited to have us and the Davis family as new neighbours, and we were excited to leave our first Apocalypse home in such eager hands.

~

Our new property on the lake was so fully treed that it wasn't set up well for animals, so Mom began the slow process of selling the remainder of our goats, sheep, chicken and geese back to local Smithers farmers. Our puppy breeding days had already come to an end after our mama springer spaniel, Olivia, had licked antifreeze off the snow the past winter and died within twenty-four hours. We kept her partner Blue, but without Olivia, his energy became hyper and aggressive. Mom sold him as soon as she could.

I really thought we would be done with animals for a while, and I looked forward to not having those affiliated chores. Our new friends, the Carson family, were about to change that, however.

The Carsons lived in a village outside of Smithers called Telkwa, on a dirt road, in a log cabin on a large property. We had met them while they were still going to the church on the hill we attended, but after they stopped going in favour of having fellowship at home, they started inviting us over to share a meal with them on Sundays.

They had eight children, aged newborn to fifteen, and approximately twenty Karelian bear dogs, from a province in Russia. They were bred specifically to protect people from bears, and they were expensive. Their kennels were spread all throughout the property, and Mr. Carson spent most of his time trying to sell them while his tired wife nursed babies and homeschooled and taught Swiss German and made every meal from scratch.

They were waiting on signs of the times too. They believed that their true home was in Eilat, Israel, and they planned on being there when Jesus returned to the Temple. They reminded me of Martin, the prophet who had spent New Year's Eve with us at the Ranch almost three years before.

I spent hours playing and learning Swiss German with all the Carson kids while Mom and Mr. Carson haggled back and forth on Bible prophecy and bear dogs. He really wanted us to buy some, since we lived in such a remote area.

"We've been there for years and only seen a bear once," my mom informed him.

"Sometimes, one bad visit is all it takes," Mr. Carson said. "If you buy two, they naturally work as a team to protect you from a bear or any other threat. They'll die for you, I promise. But you can't breed them with any other dog, the Karelian bloodline has to stay pure."

Mom reassured him that, if it ever came to that, it would not be a problem.

Now that we were animal-free and still waiting for our new cabin on McDonell Lake to be finished, Mom asked our church friends, the Dekkers, if we could stay with them for a few months. They were empty-nesting grandparents running a farm about fifteen minutes out of town on Old Babine Lake Road, so they had lots of room. We set up camp in a basement bedroom, which—to my absolute glee—had a Super Nintendo. The only issue was that their internet was still dial-up so Mom felt like she shouldn't take up their landline with her studies. She still went to town fairly often, but I was free to stay home and eat microwave burritos and play Super Mario World. The dream.

Sometimes, the Dekkers' grandson came over for a visit and played Nintendo with me. His name was Cory and he was about eight. He was bright and inquisitive and made a worthy Luigi. Sometimes his grandma Dekker would check on us to make sure we were going outside for a breath of fresh air every once in a while, and we'd head out to explore the farm.

I was always, awkwardly, ready to have a conversation about spiritual matters, so I commented that I hadn't seen Cory at our church very much.

"Yeah, we only go sometimes," he replied, kicking at the uneven dirt.

"Do you like it?" I asked.

"It's okay. Kind of boring. I like snacks and games the best."

I smiled; he reminded me of myself when I was eight, just before I'd learned how important paying attention to more than the fun stuff was.

"I get that. But it's also super amazing to know Jesus, to know that our sins can be forgiven and we can go to Heaven instead of Hell!"

Cory looked confused. "What do you mean?"

"You know, the Sinner's Prayer!"

"What's the Sinner's Prayer?"

Wow. Maybe Mom was right, and our church *did* need to focus on repentance more. How had Cory reached the age of eight without knowing about the fate of his soul? The age of ten and therefore accountability was fast approaching. This was a sign; God wanted me to save Cory.

So I excitedly told him all about the ABC's of the Sinner's Prayer, how accepting-believing-confessing led to defeating the Devil. That Jesus had suffered on the cross and gone to Hell instead of us. We needed to be grateful, we needed to worship before it was too late and the end of the world came. I pictured Cory being Left Behind next to a pile of clothes and nearly cried.

My passion was infectious, and Cory asked, "Help me pray."

It was my honour and privilege. I couldn't wait to tell my mom later that I'd saved a soul today.

~

Apparently, Cory couldn't wait to tell his mom about his soul being saved either. The very next day, she came barrelling up the long driveway in a truck and asked to talk to me.

I could tell she was unhappy, but I wasn't sure why. "Is Cory okay?"

She huffed. "Well, I don't quite know. Did you tell him about Jesus and Hell and the end of the world yesterday? Because that's all he's been talking about since he came home!"

Having another adult confront me in such a way made me feel like hiding. But as far as I was concerned, I hadn't done anything wrong. "I just told him what he needed to know to be saved and now he is! This is wonderful news!"

She seemed surprised by my boldness. "It is *my* job to walk him through that when I feel he's ready. He's only eight! These are very serious, scary things for him."

"But he's almost at the age of accountability," I stammered.

She interrupted me. "Please don't talk to him about it again."

I felt bad for Cory and his mother. They didn't know even half of what I knew when I was that age, and it had prepared me to survive however long God willed it. Maybe the world *was* coming to an end if parents didn't want their children to know how to be saved before it was too late.

Bella Coola (2003–2004)

By 2003, our new cabin on the new lake property was still not finished and Mom was convinced that where we lived at the Dekkers was not quite remote enough for the approaching Apocalypse. In her daily internet research, she had discovered a little town in BC called Bella Coola. It was more than a twelve-hour drive away, but of course she wanted to see it, so she started making plans.

My friends and their families seemed concerned but connected us with a family and the name of a church in the Bella Coola Valley for us to find refuge. In a matter of weeks, we put most of our belongings into storage over at the McDonnell Lake property, spent a few thousand dollars on two Karelian bear dogs from the Carsons for protection, purchased a rough-and-tumble Fleury RV, packed it up with the dogs and a few suitcases, and off we went.

I knew I wouldn't miss the wilderness for a single day. But leaving my two best friends, Kass and Elijah, weighed heavily on me. I knew they felt the same; they had shown me how to make an email address, and they promised to send me messages all the time. I tried to downplay the move for their sake; they hugged me tight, and I said, "My mom changes her mind about this stuff all the time. I'm sure we'll be back in a few months. Don't get your driver's licences without me," I joked.

We drove for hours, all the way down to Williams Lake. We had done this a few times before, but this time instead of continuing south toward the canyons, we went west on an unpaved road through sparse trees. On one of our few stops for gas, we saw a tourist shop with a t-shirt that said, "I Wrote My Will before I Drove the Hill."

Locals asked us where we were headed, and when we said Bella Coola, we heard more about The Hill.

For hundreds of years, there had been hunting and fishing trails made through the mountain by the Indigenous Nuxalk Peoples, but after a rush of gold and colonization by Norwegian settlers, the need for a road from the ocean to "civilization" became apparent. By 1953, the last piece of dynamite had been blown, and the road was complete. S-curving through the mountain for forty-three kilometres, starting 3,000 feet above sea level, at an 18 percent grade with no paving, no guard rails, and barely enough room to drive past another vehicle should you happen to meet one.

I was terrified; Mom was thrilled.

Slowly but surely, we made our way down the mountain, hoping and praying we weren't about to discover our hastily purchased RV didn't have good brakes. I sat by the back window, looking at the beautiful view in front of me, trying not to look down. I tried not to think about the fact that we were going somewhere we'd never been, we didn't know a single person, and we had no idea if we'd ever make our way back up this hill again.

The RV was going to be our home for the whole winter and beyond. For the past five years, I'd been waiting for an Apocalypse that had never happened, and now we were starting over again. Small seeds of anger and frustration had begun to grow in my heart, but I quashed them. This was where God had told Mom to flee; rebellion would be foolish.

When we reached the bottom of the hill, we collectively breathed a sigh of relief. The valley was narrow and dark, but the road was paved again, and close enough to see the beautifully winding Bella Coola and Nusatsum Rivers. We gratefully reached the village of Hagensborg, the home of the church we'd been told about, and also a hotel with a restaurant. It wouldn't be long before we, our transportation, and our dogs, would catch the eye of the curious locals.

~

As I had in 1998, I turned another year older in a new place before I'd really had a chance to meet anyone to celebrate with me.

I hadn't planned on turning sixteen in Bella Coola, and Mom knew I was still adjusting so she tried to make it special. In the few weeks since we'd arrived, we'd only hung out with the family that we'd been put in contact with through their cousins in Smithers.

The Daniels were another home-schooled family, on a hobby farm. Their oldest son Jeremiah was about my age, followed by six more all the way down to a newborn. They had a unique system to keep everyone in line: if mom and dad weren't around, each child could be disciplined by a sibling older than them, in a hierarchy all the way up to Jeremiah. It didn't often work, and when it did, it went to Jeremiah's head.

Mom's birthday plan was for us to bring a giant cake from the store to the Daniels's house. There was only one issue: the Daniels lived near Hagensborg, along the Nusatsum River; the only store that made giant cakes was all the way down at the shore, in Bella Coola.

So we drove the Fleury with the dogs down the highway. The plan was for me to sit on the bed and hold the cake in my lap until we got back. We were going slower than the speed limit, and several cars had to drive around us in annoyance.

Unexpectedly, we saw red and blue lights flashing behind us. "Oh shit," Mom exclaimed. "I didn't even realize they had police here. Okay, just stay back there and don't say anything, babe."

I kept my hold on the cake firm as we pulled over, my heart pounding. I wasn't sure why I was nervous; we hadn't done anything wrong... right?

"Evening," the officer said. "Licence and registration?"

Mom was ready to accommodate and handed over the papers with a smile.

"Can I ask why you were going so slow, ma'am?" he asked while rifling through the papers.

"Well, sir, it's my daughter's sixteenth birthday today, so we have a big sheet cake on her lap in the back and nowhere else to put it away from the dogs, so I just wanted to be careful."

He asked to open the Fleury side door and shone a flashlight inside to see that I was indeed the only thing protecting my cake from two Karelian bear dogs.

"No seatbelt," he gestured to me.

No real seat, I almost said, but obeying Mom, I just shrugged.

He came back around to Mom's side window. "Did you know that your registration has expired, ma'am?"

Mom gasped. "What! I checked it the other day and thought for sure I saw the end of October on there. Let me see." She took the papers back.

"It says October 7 exactly, ma'am, which is today."

Mom giggled in disbelief. "Well, shoot. You'll see we're American on the ID there. I'm so used to insurance dates going until the end of the month, I missed the '7' and assumed it meant the end of October."

"American, eh? Dual citizenship?"

"Seasonal residents," Mom countered smoothly. "We stay here for six months and go back for six months. We decided to check out this fine valley a few weeks ago."

My heart started pounding harder. My mom was lying straight to a police officer's face. I had not heard her say "seasonal resident" for years, and obviously, we had stayed put in Smithers for the past five years before this day.

"Huh. Interesting. Well, I won't ticket you this time, but I can't let you drive this vehicle any farther."

Mom got a desperate tone in her voice. "This is our only vehicle and it's my daughter's birthday. People are waiting for us to bring this cake right now. Can't you make an exception? I'll go take care of this insurance first thing tomorrow."

"Sorry, ma'am. Where are you heading, though? I can give you a ride."

"Oh, thank you!" Mom exclaimed. The officer left to go open his back doors, and Mom started gathering up our things in a fluster.

"Mom," I whispered. "Why did you lie?"

Her eyes cut to me quickly. "You remember that scene at the end of the *Sound of Music*? Where the nuns stole the car parts from those Nazis and lied about hiding the Von Trapp family? This is kind of like that. Sometimes, it's okay to lie, especially if it keeps others safe. Today, that's us. Now get the dogs and stay quiet."

I handed my cake to the officer, who put it in his front seat, and then Mom and I awkwardly folded ourselves into the back with the dogs on our laps. In their anxiety, they immediately peed on us, and I didn't blame them. The back of the car was completely boxed in, glass separating from the front, and adult-proof locks on the door handles. It evoked shame and punishment, even though I wasn't sure I deserved it.

The fifteen-minute remainder of our drive felt squished and endless. When we finally pulled into the Daniels's driveway, I breathed a sigh of relief. The whole family poured out of the house to greet us; I guess they'd never seen a police car in their driveway before.

"What did you do?" Jeremiah laughed, taking the cake from me.

I don't know, I thought. *I don't know.*

~

Once again, attending a local church would prove to be the common denominator that connected us to everything else in a new town. Hagensborg was a few kilometres east of the Nuxalk reserve in Bella Coola and the ocean; it had a hotel, a restaurant, a school, and a church based out of a house. James and Connie lived in the house, and ran weekly ministries there, but every Sunday morning, the service was led by a woman in her late fifties named Nina. Mom, and therefore I, didn't know how she felt about Nina being the sole head of this Body, but she also allowed that in such a remote place, you do what you can with what (or who) you have. God would have to sort the rest.

The feelings of déjà vu continued. Church every Sunday, sometimes opened with the blowing of the shofar—followed by a meal with various families, Mom educating everyone around her about the future, drawing in many and alienating others... again. We rumbled around the narrow valley in the Fleury, scoping out our new world. We found waterfalls and totem poles and houses in haphazard rows, and one rare little Internet café that worked most of the time. We predictably spent so much time there, Mom was eventually asked to be in charge of running the café for the locals. She took the post in a heartbeat, and I started occasionally babysitting for young church families, saving up my money—for what, I wasn't sure.

Our Karelian bear dogs, bred to be freely following their instincts around the countryside, were regularly cooped up and grumpy. We would often spend the day out and return to our RV filled with dogshit and piss soaking through the plywood floor. That smell never came out.

I was constantly annoyed by this, and yet I admired the dogs. They were upset, and they had very few ways of expressing it. I wished I was bold enough to communicate my feelings about being uprooted and displaced again, but instead I poured my energy into talking with Kass and Elijah on MSN Messenger and writing on Christian youth forums. I found camaraderie with angry and sad young people halfway across the world who wondered why it felt like Jesus wasn't enough anymore; I felt like I could share this with internet strangers more honestly than I could with anyone I knew in person.

~

Even though I had failed miserably in my piano lessons with Sharon back in Smithers, I still wanted to learn how to play piano, to lead in worship. At the home church, if no one else was around, I would sit at the keyboard. I would listen to each note, and I memorized what each chord was made of, so if a simple piece of sheet music said "G D Em C," I already had the muscle memory pattern loaded up in my fingers. I taught myself the entire board, sharps and flats. After many hours and days spent sitting, I could play just about any key and I wouldn't get dizzy. I could even sing at the same time. I realized that my issue boiled down to something like knowing how to read but not being able to spell. Each individual "letter" on traditional sheet music was too much to process, but chords were words made up of those letters, stacked. Maybe I wasn't smart, but I was resourceful, and maybe that would be enough to succeed.

~

I unexpectedly felt some peace and curiosity when I spent time on the Nuxalk reserve. Some of the Indigenous families went to the home church, but sometimes they chose to attend a potlatch ceremony or, depending on the time of year, went fishing for oolichan whose meat and oil would help them thrive in the coming winter. In this isolated place, most traditions had prevailed; it created a culture of slowing down, spending time together and talking all day while getting important tasks done. Time meant nothing, and family meant everything.

Mom was friendly enough with Nuxalk people (she saw some future benefit to how they preserved food for survival) but tried to be very careful about how much time I was spending with them. She said that even though there were a lot of Christians living there, they still held to some influences of demons, potlatch being one of them. And when they prepared their fish, not only did they thank God the Creator for the fish, they thanked the actual fish for giving its life.

"It's unnecessary," she said. "It's pagan animism; you can't mix the sacred with the profane, but some people still try. Use wisdom."

I nodded, but I was confused. She had said that I was a Yaqui Indian like my dad when I was a kid—did they live like this too? It didn't seem that wrong. The fish *had* given its life, after all, and we benefited by continuing to live after we ate them; it seemed almost rude not to thank them. Surely, Jesus, of all people—fisherman *and* life-giver—could not see anything profane in the practice of thanking a sacrifice.

But God was a jealous God, and to Him belonged *all* the glory. I knew this, and He knew better than I.

~

Over the 2003–2004 winter, we found enough house-sitting jobs to stay warm, thanks to folks who always left the Valley for open spaces and warmer climates. I got used to the comfort of sleeping in my own room again, and watching movies the homeowners already had or renting them from the corner section in one of the two grocery stores. After I got tired of watching all the Bible movies and *Left Behind* series, I begged Mom to be allowed to watch *Pirates of the Caribbean* and *Lord of the Rings*. She finally said yes, to my delight. I was growing up.

This opened a door, however. Pirates and elves led to *The Mask of Zorro* and *The Mummy.* Everyone was so heroic and pretty; watching the men made me feel strong, but watching the women made me feel tingly, like I was anticipating a tickle fight. In the limitations of my awkward, confused, gangly body, all I wanted was to have long flowing hair, wear bodices, study books and defeat enemies with swords next to Elizabeth Swan, Arwen of Rivendell, Elena De la Vega and Evelyn O'Connell. I would never tell anyone that, though. It felt… wrong. Too close to worldly feminism and something else I couldn't quite put my finger on.

Mom enjoyed these movies too, although she wasn't too keen on magic and zombies. She had really enjoyed *Gladiator* and Russell Crowe, so when *A Beautiful Mind* was released, she rented it for us one weekend. You can imagine my surprise when I immediately felt kinship with John Forbes Nash Jr. and his paranoid distrust of the government—only to discover that he had been seeing things the whole time. Twist of the century, to me. I had to look up his story on the internet later just to make sure that was how it actually ended because Mom and I had spent the last ten minutes of that movie waiting for the *other* twist, that he hadn't actually been mentally ill, they just wanted him to think he was to discredit him. But no, it had been a true story. The government being out to get someone has often been the case, but not here.

I thought about how we were spending our first winter in such a remote place, a place that would require outside intervention if natural disasters or otherwise were to occur. It was Mom's idea of safety to be so cut off, and in fact, she had cautioned all of our friends that if anything were to threaten the Valley (Bella Coola being somewhere between a fault line and the sea), we should not comply with evacuation protocols. People like us disappeared with no explanation, she believed. If it was "our time," then it was our time.

But what if help was just... help?

What if the second twist was just a creation of our beautiful minds?

~

We spent the remainder of winter house-sitting, and then during what was spring break for those kids who were attending school, I got invited to spend some time back in Smithers with the Marshall family. Luckily, a friend in Bella Coola was driving to Williams Lake and they were able to give me a ride. I caught a bus to Smithers from there, the slowly chugging wheels feeling like they would never make it there.

But they did. I spent a week at my favourite house, skiing and eating and watching movies, feeling completely independent and free. No Bible debates or Apocalypse arguments, just peace.

The day before I took the bus back to Williams Lake, Elijah took me to the Zellers a few blocks away from his house. I had brought all my saved-up babysitting money with me, and I'd mentioned I was thinking about getting a camera. I didn't know if I had enough for one, but Elijah said he would help me shop for it.

We went through the automatic doors and straight to the Photography section. I felt like a child seeing a magic trick for the first time when Elijah showed me something called a digital camera. It took pictures that you could see on a screen immediately after you took them. *These must be brand new*, I thought.

"These types have been out for a couple of years now," the salesman said. "If you get a SIM card, you can have way more storage, and then it can be inserted directly into your computer to upload images."

I delicately held the tiny square chip between my thumb and finger like it was a priceless diamond. "Well, this is going to be a lot harder to keep track of than a floppy disk," I said. Elijah smirked, which made me happy.

I handed over all two hundred of my hard-earned dollars after Elijah said that was a really good deal; the whole walk home, I felt stunned that I'd actually made such a purchase. My long-held wish of being able to document everything around me before it all came to an end—if it was ever actually going to—was finally in my hands. I took pictures with my friends that night before I left Smithers, and I already knew which waterfall I wanted to capture when I got back to Bella Coola. My mom was going to be impressed.

~

For the rest of spring and summer of 2004, we lived in a bed and breakfast along Highway 20, in exchange for cleaning the rooms, mowing the grounds, and my assistance in the kitchen. My pillowy French bread became the daily demand of fishers, hunters and hikers who were about to spend the entire day outside. Mom taught me how to scrub a sink until it shone and make a bed with the precision of a seamstress. Elbow grease, I learned, was the key.

I also stayed busy babysitting a one-year-old baby boy while his mama was starting her very own café and art gallery down the road. He had dark hair and delicious cheeks, and the way he used ASL with his sausage roll hands to communicate what he wanted made me feel something I hadn't felt before. Maybe it was the innocent way that he saw the world. Maybe it was hope that one day, I could have my own child after all, and be a good mama that wasn't afraid all the time.

I enjoyed having a roof over my head and some regular money in my pocket, but I longed for Smithers. Coming back to Bella Coola after spring break had felt like splitting myself in half all over again. The narrow Valley felt like it inched closer to my lungs every day, and I fled to the ocean whenever I could.

By August, I was done. It had been almost a year since we left the Bulkley Valley and the wilderness, and I was spending every spare minute I could at the Internet café, listening to Relient K on the K-Love radio station and emailing my Smithers friends. They missed me. The youth group there had a new youth pastor and was starting a ministry team; they wanted me to be a part of it. After weeks of playing piano every Sunday at the Hagensborg home church for a generation that really only liked songs I didn't know, this possibility felt fresh and exciting.

So one evening, Mom and I had dinner at the Bella Coola Valley Inn, and I decided to play the God card.

"I know you feel God led us here, and I respect that. But I really believe that God is about to do amazing things with the youth group back in Smithers, and they've asked me to come join them. I can stay with friends. This place just feels like a dead-end to me, and I need to breathe, so I don't really care how I get out of here but I'm going." I tried to make my sixteen-year-old voice sound as authoritative as possible, certain the hammer was about to come down on my rebellious spirit.

But to my complete surprise, Mom agreed. We made plans to start packing up and leaving before winter, but I looked for every opportunity to leave sooner.

As luck would have it, Pastor Nina's son Dave lived in Smithers with his family, and he frequently made helicopter trips back and forth doing supply runs for his fishing lodge on the Dean River. About a week after I gave Mom my "ultimatum," Dave flew in, made his deliveries, and invited me to take the flight back with him in his empty chopper.

I never packed a backpack so quickly in my life.

I phoned Elijah to say I would be home in the next few hours, threw my backpack in the back, and put on a seatbelt with a headset. Mom kissed me and hugged me tight, saying she would see me as soon as possible. "Don't eat too much of other people's food, and clean up after yourself," she reminded me. Of course, I reassured her.

I watched the beautiful, claustrophobic Valley become smaller and smaller until it disappeared; my face felt like it might crack with how wide my smile was.

Halfway through the two-hour flight, Dave swooped low over a snow-covered mountain and pointed toward my window. I gasped; a wild elk, or maybe a caribou, was running through the snow just below me. With my new camera I took a picture that would never do it justice, and Dave resumed altitude, the small helicopter wiggling in the wind a bit. I didn't care. Whether we crashed or landed, I was free.

Take Your Own Life

I wish the words "take your own life"
Didn't have to mean death by suicide
Because most days I don't wanna die
I just wanna take my own life
Back
From the men
From the church
From my mom
From the voice inside my head
That speaks in all their dulcet tones
That says I'll never be good
But keep trying

Return to Smithers (2004–2006)

Even though I lived in Bella Coola for only a year, the youth group I returned to in Smithers felt different. We were meeting multiple times a week —Wednesdays for ministry team practice, and Fridays for services. By early September, the ministry team was already in full swing so that we could bring the Gospel in fun, innovative ways to people outside the church.

A few weeks after my helicopter flight, Mom, the bear dogs and the old Fleury motorhome rumbled back into town. We stayed in the Dekkers's basement out of town again while we tried to find a more permanent place to live.

During the long winter months, GLO (God Loving Others!) would get together on Wednesday nights and practise our various skills. Singing, playing instruments, reading the Bible intuitively and praying, Drime (a fancy word for a dialogueless, heavily thematic skit acted out to emotionally influential music), altar calls, equipment set up and take down—everyone had a job to do, and by the time summer came, we were ready for Sunday mornings and sleepaway camp and Vacation Bible School. We all looked forward to the May long weekend when we would pile into a school bus and drive for twelve hours down to desert-like Kamloops. It was a long-standing tradition to attend an event called History Maker, a youth convention where we could be spiritually refreshed and feel God light the fire in our hearts for Him again.

I spent much of my weekend in Kamloops feeling ill at ease, wanting to crawl out of my skin, without knowing why. During worship services, I often wept as I had visions of being surrounded by fire, seeing hands reach up from the flames, begging to be rescued. Not being able to save any of them, I was filled with the kind of guilt that made me devote myself to Jesus even more.

I had no idea that the arena which was filled with thousands of youth from all over the province gathered to worship God and speak in tongues and pray was mere kilometres away from the residential school where the bones of hundreds of Indigenous youth who wanted to speak their own tongue, who prayed to go home, were put in the ground by God's supposed chosen. My body knew before I did. We never learned about them in our schools, in our churches, in our History Maker conventions. We would go home, full of ideas about how to bring Jesus to *our* schools.

We were aged thirteen to seventeen and already our mission was political. We vied for our pastors' and leaders' attention, practising everything we knew, hoping that their light would shine on us with a kind word and promotion. Lead worship, lead Drime creator, lead in how many souls we could bring into the kingdom. We learned how to Share Jesus Without Fear (read: consent), counting on the Holy Spirit to do its gentle work, like hot soapy water working at the stains. Well done, good and faithful servant. You have pleased the Father enough to keep Hell at bay for a little while longer.

After leaving Bella Coola, I was keen on joining the ministry. I had taught myself to play almost any worship song on the keyboard, I could sing, I discovered I enjoyed acting. Maybe leading people to Christ could be fun.

The new youth pastor, Rob, recognized my fresh blood, so he gave me plenty to do. I was so earnest I didn't even see how it drove a wedge between my best friend, Kass, and me for nearly a whole year after I returned.

I had spent weekends and holidays at her house for years, and as we grew, it became apparent how different we were. Kass was pretty and popular with a rebellious streak; she could drive and watch *Harry Potter* and go to parties with non-Christian high school boys. She was allowed to wear what I thought were form-fitting jeans with spaghetti strap tank tops. She confided in me the stories of wild things that happened at those parties, and I mistook it for intimacy and trust. She and another boy on the ministry team coupled up pretty quickly, and my worry about her shifted to a DEFCON 1. I knew I had to do something when I kept accidentally discovering them completely alone, behind closed doors, in situations that made me blush.

I tried to talk to her, to no avail. I went to her parents, as I thought was biblically appropriate.

Her mom, who had always been warm and welcoming with me, invited me out to coffee at Kokopelli's. I thought she would be thankful that I cared enough about her daughter to say something, but instead, she told me that I was acting out of jealousy since I didn't have a boyfriend and I should leave her daughter alone. After all, I was the one who'd taken her place on the ministry team while she graciously said nothing.

The situation came to a head when Pastor Rob made plans to move to another province, to help another church. We all wept, Kass particularly, wondering how we would carry on. Surely, this could not be God's plan.

One bombshell after another fell as he also announced that he'd appointed one of our oldest ministry team members, Mandie, to fill in for him until an official youth pastor could replace him. It had been assumed that Kass's mom and dad would take over, but Pastor Rob had changed his mind at the last minute.

Hell hath no fury like an ambitious pair of church parents who've worked hard, been good, and then denied their promotion without warning. Our ministry team, youth group, and the church itself began bleeding as gossip and rumours and confrontations spread. After the worldliness I'd seen displayed in my friend and her parents, I was vocal about honouring our departing pastor's wishes and standing behind our new leader.

I was maligned, pulled aside into "meetings," reprimanded, asked to clarify what I really meant, and told that my "artistically vibrant imagination" might have led me to misunderstand the entire situation. Shame and anxiety were almost constant; Mom gave me her blessing to leave if they were going to be such "snakes in the grass."

Elijah, who was allergic to conflict, seemed worried about me and just wanted things to go back to the way they were before.

Mandie got so stressed out that she distanced herself from the church entirely. She started dating a non-Christian she worked with in town, got pregnant, and needed to take a leave of absence from all of us. This was the fate I wanted to save Kass from; I knew she didn't want to become a mom at seventeen, and that was the only acceptable option for good girls like us who were pregnant.

Kass's parents were waiting in the wings as soon as Mandie left, and our head pastor took it upon himself to preach from the pulpit about forgiveness, reconciliation, unity, healing. He appointed and blessed our new leaders officially; those of us still in the ministry team were expected to fall in line, and we did. Swallowing the bitter taste in our mouths, we moved on, even though I felt like the curtain in front of what this church was actually like was starting to be pulled back. It seemed like a power trip, and I wasn't interested. But I still believed the kingdom of Heaven was at stake, so I stayed.

By the time 2005 ended, Kass broke up with her boyfriend and we made amends. Our friendship was good for a while, spending our nights at the movie theatre, going through the McDonald's drive-thru late at night and singing Linkin Park at the top of our lungs. Kass once again trusted me to hold all her angry secrets, and I prayed for her every night. It felt right to be in her atmosphere again. But inevitably, a new boyfriend would come along and she'd disappear.

Kass's mom's affection for me was no longer through gritted teeth; she was glad I'd stuck around long enough to hopefully influence her daughter to stay on the path of least rebellion. I tried my best, but I was beginning to tire of policing the souls of others. Had God not given us free will for a reason?

~

Now that we had decided we were going to stay in the town of Smithers for the immediate future, in the fall of 2005 (after spending a year house-sitting and staying in the Dekkers's basement), Mom found a tiny one-bedroom shack five minutes out of town near Lake Kathlyn to rent for a good price. We still had most of our possessions in storage on our other property on McDonell Lake, so Mom made negotiations to sell that to the tourists who had purchased our first property the year before. By this time, the Davis family had left Copper River Ranch, and we no longer felt a connection to survive the Apocalypse there.

Mom would keep an eye on things from the Internet café in town; one day while she was out driving, she asked the Lord, "if we need to flee by 2008, show me a sign." A moment later, a black bear crossed the road right in front of her, and she seemed content with that. Almost three years to rest and prepare.

Since I was on my way to seventeen, she wanted me to feel like I had some privacy, so she let me have the bedroom. She put her bed out in the corner of the living room, and we filled our space with appliances from Canadian Tire. After so many years off-the-grid, or using other folks' amenities, it felt downright odd to buy everyday items that needed electrical outlets. To have a fridge, and food that could last longer than a day. We still shunned having a TV but went to the movie theatre on the one-way street every once in a while.

Out in the small, overgrown yard, the Karelian bear dogs were thrilled to finally have a bit of space within their fences. Mom wanted to fix up the Fleury after the dogs had destroyed it, so she would invite my friends over on Saturday afternoons to clean and paint. Then she'd order a pizza and give them cash for their trouble.

Life took a strange turn when my friends started getting their first jobs at fast food places, saving up money to buy their first second-hand car. Some of them were old enough to drive by themselves but couldn't pick me up without having another adult present. I didn't really question it much, though; I was just happy to have a ride to church and youth group after Mom had decided our church wasn't focussing enough on repentance and hellfire for her to continue going.

"Didn't you turn sixteen a while ago? Why don't you have your driver's licence yet?" Adults and youth alike would ask me. I would shrug and say I hadn't tried yet; why would I need to when I'd known how to drive for five years already?

But the idea of having a job and saving up some money, having a bit more freedom appealed to me greatly. I asked my friends how they'd gotten started, and they said they took their identification to provincial insurance at ICBC, and whatever jobs were hiring. Some of them had taken a Work Experience course for a semester at the high school.

Well, that sounded easy enough.

I asked Mom for any identification she thought I'd need. Her brow furrowed slightly. "It might take me a while to find it, and I'm not sure how things work here."

But after I kept begging, she found my Social Security card. "I can't find your birth certificate, but you shouldn't need that to get a job or drive," she said confidently.

McDonald's was nearly always hiring, so I went to the front counter and asked for an application. I smiled as I filled it out, leaving a couple lines blank that I wasn't sure about.

When the manager saw it, she paused. "Okay, we just need your SIN card and we should be all set."

I stared at her blankly.

"Your social insurance card? Do you know the number? It's just for tax purposes, everyone has one."

"Oh, my mom probably forgot to give it to me, I'll come back with it," I stammered awkwardly. I never went back.

It was the same story at ICBC. I couldn't take a driver's licence test without some kind of identification card with a number. I thought it was extremely silly; obviously I existed, I was right in front of them! I could work hard and drive well, I just needed a chance to show them.

(When our youth group signed up to be counsellors for kids at summer Bible camps, I couldn't get a criminal background check either. But somehow, they made that go away, and I was allowed to shape young minds for the Lord anyway.)

After some months of confusion and prayer, I came back to Mom. "So I think I'm gonna need a social insurance card and a care card to really get anywhere. Can you help me?"

Mom's face became serious. "Babe, you know as well as I do that the government wants to be up in our business, especially after 9/11. It's absolutely immoral that they're trying to force this on you."

I nodded. "Yeah, it's pretty silly. But it shouldn't be hard to do, right? I'm almost eighteen and I really wanna work and drive with my friends."

What she said next made a weird pit land in my stomach even though I didn't fully understand it.

"When I drove us up here eight years ago, I didn't think all of this would still be here. My timing for the prophecies must have been off somewhere, or maybe the Lord is giving us more time. But when we crossed the border, we didn't need any papers other than to say we were seasonal residents, at the time."

"What does 'seasonal resident' mean?" I asked. I vaguely remembered the night of my sixteenth birthday and the lies she'd told the police officer who'd helped deliver us, my cake, and the dogs to the Daniels's house.

"It's what folks do when they want to travel back and forth to avoid the snow. You stay for six months, and then you go back for six months, and the border keeps signing your papers."

The wheels were starting to turn in my brain. "But… we didn't do that. We just… stayed."

Mom tried to act nonchalant. "Well, like I said, I thought all of this was going to disappear and there would be no need for paperwork. It's going to be 2008 in two years anyway, which is when the Lord has told me it's time to flee, so if we can just wait a little while longer, we'll be okay."

I swallowed hard. "Okay, I guess so, but… what do I do instead? And what if the prophecy is wrong again? Then I can do the paperwork?"

Mom smiled. "You're so smart and hardworking, you'll figure something out. Babysitting, house-sitting, cleaning. Maybe you can invent something! There's lots to do out there that doesn't require paperwork, babe."

"So I do that for two years and then what?"

"Even if my calculation is off again—which it shouldn't be—I don't think doing the paperwork is wise. The government won't understand why we haven't done it yet, and they'll probably put us in jail. And we'll never be seen again! So you can't tell anyone, do you understand? Just ask for jobs around town that will pay you cash. That's it."

"But—"

Mom put her hand up. "That's it! We have to trust God like we always have! I've been able to stretch out my family inheritance this far and we are going to be fine until money becomes worthless. Then we have the rest of our gold and silver."

I tried to hide the tears of frustration in my eyes. "Okay."

After that, I'm not sure what got better: my ability to lie, or my friends' ability to stop asking questions.

High School (2006–2007)

To me, living off-the-grid, in that cabin for over four years had been enough waiting for the Apocalypse. Perhaps my mother was right and the Apocalypse was coming in 2008: but she'd also taught me to "hope for the best, and prepare for the worst."

For me, "the worst" was no longer the world ending—it was being an adult in a world that kept spinning, with no resources to survive. I could no longer justify wasting time on a "what if."

Out of respect for my mother and my own confusion about my identification, I decided I would live my life as best I could with the restrictions that my lack of identification allowed—while I figured out what to do about that identification.

I became the most available girl in the world for anything anyone needed, as long as it paid in cash. I was the babysitter for kids, house-sitter for pets, gardens and more. Because I had gained experience cleaning the lodge in Bella Coola, I knew the best money was in cleaning houses: ten dollars an hour. But not many Smithers folks were the type to outsource their house cleaning, and most businesses used an official company.

I was ready to grow up and plan for a future. I realized that if I was to have any success, including inventing something like Mom had suggested, I would need to know more shit about things. All of my good friends, two years younger than me, were about to graduate high school—and I hadn't cracked open a schoolbook in over five years.

I started hanging out at Smithers Senior Secondary slowly, first at lunchtime. The cafeteria was like a dome full of round tables; its entrance doubled as the doorway to the Della Herman Theatre where the school put on musicals every other year, and travelling acts entertained the Valley.

For five days a week, I'd spend an hour laughing around the table with my friends. Sometimes I had my own food, sometimes I didn't. The best day was Tuesday; we'd walk a little path through the woods that came out at a highway intersection featuring a Kal Tire and a KFC/Taco Bell on the way out of town. On Tuesdays, tacos were three-for-five-dollars and half the high school would show up. The cost equal to an hour of babysitting—I could do that. If we were lucky, we'd have a chance to sit down and actually eat before the lunch hour was over. And then the bell would ring, and we'd take off, but instead of going to class, I'd go to the school library.

The office receptionists and the librarians started to know me by name. And of course, they asked questions. Questions that I think I secretly hoped an adult would ask so that they'd figure out I needed help.

By the spring of 2006, I had dropped enough clues to my inside women about my situation that they started to give advice. Turns out that lots of kids had grown up home-schooled in the Valley and were in need of an official diploma. Turns out that lots of foreign exchange students attended the high school before their paperwork was officially filed.

I made an appointment with a school counsellor, and she was extremely helpful.

"You'll be nineteen this year?" She asked while typing.

"In October," I replied.

"So it looks like you'd be eligible for the Adult Dogwood diploma. It's for older students like yourself who maybe dropped out or are catching up. The only issue is that you wouldn't be eligible for any bursaries or scholarships to other schools."

"Oh, that's okay!" I said, hope starting to fill my heart. I wouldn't be needing any of those.

"And you said you're from the US, but your paperwork isn't finalized yet?"

"Yes, it might be another year," I lied easily.

"That's all right. If it gets to graduation time and your papers still aren't through, all you have to do is pay for the courses you took." She handed me a list of the courses required to graduate and their cost.

I'd cross that bridge when I came to it.

~

I did another summer of "criminal background check ignored" counselling at Summer Bible Camp, and started buying school supplies for the first time in over a decade. I couldn't stop smiling. Mom was nervous but she was happy for me. "I'm very proud of you for showing initiative and finding a way to make this work," she said. "I knew you were smart."

The youth group was excited that yet another young person passionate for the Lord was going to be joining the student ranks. But I'd already made the decision to reach as many people with love as I could, without evangelizing or mentioning Jesus or the Apocalypse at all. If they asked, I'd tell them, of course. But the most important thing—in fact, what I believed God wanted from me now—was to focus on studying and personal growth alone. I trusted that my light would shine bright enough to anyone who wanted to be found.

To graduate, I only needed twenty credits, and eight of those were required to be English 12 and Math 12. My expertise in Math had not increased with time, but thankfully we found a compromise: Math Essentials 11 could still count toward graduation, and it focussed more on how to file taxes or buy a car.

The other three courses needed were elective. Since my mom was definitely going to be paying for this by the end of the year, I decided to treat myself to eight, a full thirty-two credit course load. English, Math, History, Computer, Textiles, Choir, Theatre, and Work Experience. I might never invent something, but I was on the verge of re-inventing myself.

I think I was the only grade twelve high school student that was actually excited to be there. My energy was a bit like that of an alarm clock playing "Walking on Sunshine" to someone who'd been up all night. I was a good song, I just failed to read the room.

But underneath my excitement was a deep fear that I was going to be found out, federally and academically. The school counsellor had said her door was open anytime if I found myself struggling with the educational jump to grade twelve from... whatever I'd been doing. I completely appreciated her, and after being around mostly adults my entire life, I was very comfortable asking teachers about anything I didn't understand.

It turns out I already knew a lot of things in practice (thanks to my reading habits)—I just didn't know what those things were called. My binders were full of notes I'd been taking since the moment I stepped into my first homeroom, and I got lost trying to find my locker only a couple of times.

I could write about something I'd read in English 12 easily, I just needed to know what an essay format was. Thankfully, my teacher was an understanding man, and he loved giving handouts on all things English 12 Terms. After a decade of reading mostly Christian End Times or Purity Culture books disguised as romance novels, I enjoyed reading and writing about *All Quiet on the Western Front* and *The Alchemist* and watching *Twelve Angry Men* the most. I still don't get Shakespeare.

I soaked in every bit of History 12, but my memory wasn't always the best and covering World War I all the way to the first Iraq War was... a lot. Especially when my only previous experience with World History was the Christian Abeka curriculum—which can basically be summed up into "America good, everyone else bad, God said so, we win." My teacher was a smart, kind man who shattered that imperialist glass for me a little more with every maze-like explanation he wrote on the whiteboard.

With Textiles, Computer and Math Essentials... let's just say I faked it until I made it, and I have one pair of poorly made penguin-print pajama pants to show for it. They're splitting apart and they'll never fit me again, but at the very back of my drawer they'll stay until they are threads.

For Work Experience, I chose to intern at the local newspaper, *The Interior News*. I spent a few hours there every Saturday for that term and I loved it. I reported for local town events and school events, and I learned to take short-hand notes that still made sense to me. My personality was jovial and while I wasn't always sure if I was asking the right questions, I took pleasure in doing interviews with Smithers locals. I wish I'd kept track of every article that was printed with my name in the byline, proof that I had indeed been there. My boss, the editor-in-chief, said he'd be happy to write a letter of recommendation if I ever wanted to go to journalism school, which surprised me. He had my gratitude and my deeply hidden disappointment that this would never be my fate. Cinderella was only going to be in this world long enough to steal a shoe and run.

I thrived in Choir, naturally, and in Theatre, all it took was a little prompting from my teacher to blossom. It was indeed what my religious indoctrination called a "slippery slope," however. Mom liked to call it Incrementalism, which is the concept that following Jesus was on the straight and narrow way, but the world was on a broad highway. Anything goes! And each step you take that leads you onto the wider, easier path—even though it feels good—eventually leads to Hell. I'd been aware of guarding my heart from the dangers of going to a public high school, but Theatre is where I was truly tested.

Not only did I become accustomed to learning dance choreography with boys and doing quick costume changes in the wings no matter who was there with me—but I became a witch.

In the winter-spring of 2007, our theatre procured the rights to perform *Scots on the Rocks (A Parody of Macbeth)* by Richard Nathan. It is quite a funny script, and since the costuming was bound to be rather modest, I auditioned for a role where I would have one scene and then die offstage. I studied my monologue voraciously and I thought it went well.

But after all the auditions were done, Heather—she wasn't like a regular teacher, she was a cool teacher, so we all called her by her first name—pulled me aside.

Swallowing the ever-present fear that I was in trouble for some reason, I sat down with her.

"You had a great audition, Carly. But I think you can do better. How would you like to be one of the three witches?"

My swallow of fear turned into one of shock. That was a main role. It involved singing and dancing and being deliciously nasty.

I found myself caught between possibly disappointing my teacher and disappointing my Father in Heaven.

I looked Heather right in the eye and said, "I'll have to pray about it."

And pray I did, for a whole weekend. By the following Monday, I had decided that God knew about acting. And he knew my heart too. This was *Macbeth*, for crying out loud. The spells weren't even real—not like *Harry Potter* (or so I'd been told). I could be careful and make a good memory. If Heather believed in me, then it'd be silly not to believe in myself, right?

And so Spell-Witch I became. I spent every waking hour at the theatre and became good friends with my fellow witches; we practised choreography and I wrote music. I painted my skin green and teased my hair and wore a black dress with slits up the side and down the front. I learned how to hide inside a giant cauldron as it rolled out onto the stage, to gracefully climb out of it, to stand on the edges and sing while it was still moving. I drew a mascara moustache onto Lady Macbeth's face and "changed" her into a man without blinking an eye. I received standing ovations and a "Best Supporting Actress" certificate, and I had the literal God-damned time of my life.

~

Before I knew it, my whirlwind high school education was drawing to a close—but it still held a few surprises for me. I had thoroughly enjoyed prom after borrowing a dress from a church friend and inviting a young man from Theatre to attend with me. (He was two grades younger than me, but the only boy I felt safe and comfortable dancing with, so his parents signed a permission slip and off we went!) Now, it was June, and time to get ready for graduation.

My choir teacher Mr. Doogan-Smith asked me to stay after class one afternoon; he told me that he'd really enjoyed my musical performances throughout the year, and wondered if I'd not only like to open the graduation ceremonies by leading the national anthem but *also* choose a song to perform that represented the whole graduating class of 2007.

My mouth nearly fell open. "I'd be honoured to do one or the other, but surely there are other choir students who have been here longer who'd like to sing too?"

Doogie (as we all called him) looked at me thoughtfully. "If you really don't want to, that's all right, I just think you're the right person for the job."

Once again, I was faced with the choice between possibly disappointing a teacher and possibly falling headlong into failure. Well, the dream year I'd been pinching myself about was nearly at an end, and I'd rather die than not go out with a bang.

This last task would require one last bout of homework. After living in Canada for almost ten years, I only slightly knew the anthem.

After consulting Google, I practised every day. In my head, I heard "our home on native land" even while singing "and." It didn't seem like a big deal to me, it just made sense.

Once I felt confident I'd memorized the words to the anthem, it didn't take long for me to choose a grad class song. One of my very favourite country music artists, Martina McBride, had released a new song called "Anyway" that had become my own personal anthem as I contemplated a new kind of future.

I spent hours in the music room, piecing together enough chords to give the song the glorious sound it deserved, and once I knew it, I asked a fellow grad student to play bass guitar with me at the ceremony; he picked it up right away. (Doogie had offered to play piano for the anthem so I didn't have to worry about that, thankfully.)

Graduation season in Canada is a little odd, honestly. I'd gotten used to the schedule continuing into June instead of ending in May like America did, but it felt pretty anticlimactic to have prom lead into grad weekend, and then come back to school on Monday for two and a half more weeks of class. Still, I was determined to celebrate.

The Smithers Civic Centre Arena is where most of the big events in town are held. A few weeks before, it had been transformed into a "James Bond 007" theme (because it was 2007, get it?) for prom, and now the floor was lined with row after row of chairs with an aisle down the middle and a stage at one end. Almost like a concert. I started getting nervous. Not only would I have to make it down the elevated platform of the aisle without falling, but these chairs and stands would be packed. I was about to sing and play the piano in front of a few thousand people—most of whom barely knew my name.

But I had time. We were directed to line up in alphabetical order at the back of the arena, and it didn't take too long to get to the Bs. I walked down the aisle to many cheers, paused for a picture at the end of the aisle, and made it to my seat on the stage successfully. Now all I had to do was wait.

After all the grads A to Z found their seats, my stomach started flip-flopping a bit. Moments later, my name was called, and I shakily made my way through everyone's knees to go stand beside Doogie at the piano. I invited everyone to stand, and then I sang Canada's national anthem without a single mistake. Well, perhaps just one: The front page of the newspaper the following week featured a picture of me, decked in royal blue, with my hand over my heart like a damn American. No one told me to do it, no one told me not to do it. It is just one of those things I will always giggle about because no one in that entire arena except my proud mother knew the secret that I was the least Canadian grad to ever Canuck, and I almost gave it all away.

Grad ceremonies are long. There's just no other way to say it. There are so many people, teachers and grads to honour—everyone gets their moment in the sun. Including me. About halfway through the ceremony, my name was called again. Suddenly, I realized that the attendees were shrouded in darkness; the only people I could actually see was my grad class, and I wasn't nervous anymore. They'd heard me sing many times, and this was for them. It was my last chance to leave an impression on them, to let them know how much I appreciated them and how loved they were.

On the ego side, a singer's voice never sounds better than it does into a crisp hot microphone in a full arena, I'm sure of it. I rode the high of my own sound, my class's standing ovation, and the proud emotion of my mom and my friends' parents for days after that.

My tassels had been flipped, my new friends had cried into my hair, my Adult Dogwood Diploma was tucked safely under my arm. I did it. I fucking did it, all by myself, with no one the wiser.

Or so I thought.

A few weeks after graduation, when the last class had finished, Mom went into the office to pay for my year like we'd agreed to. She came home with a perplexed look on her face.

"Carly... you said you weren't eligible for any bursaries or scholarships in your class, right?"

I nodded, not looking up from my book.

"Well, somebody paid for you before I got there."

Now I was paying attention. "*What?*"

"I went into the office with my chequebook, and the receptionist said it had already been taken care of by a person who wanted to remain anonymous and wished you all the best."

I was stunned. We had previously calculated that with my choir and theatre trips to Edmonton and Peachland, my graduation year would cost us at least two thousand dollars, and that was on the low side. Mom had been fully supportive about paying it, but it would have been a huge blow to our family savings.

It's been sixteen years since I graduated, and to this day, I still have no idea who saw me, who figured me out, who had that kind of money just sitting around to spend on me.

I owe them everything.

In that moment, I felt that Jesus had come through for me through the kindness of the stranger, maybe even what my mom called a "God Thing." God wanted me to graduate high school. Maybe I didn't need to be set apart, like Mom said. Maybe I could be a part of the future.

Moving Out (2008)

I had devoted ten months of my life to education and, against all odds, pulled it off. The future was still feeling a little muddy to me, though. What was the next best step? This kind of situation wasn't exactly laid out in the Bible to follow. I decided to wait and see what 2008 was going to hold, if anything.

Life returned to normal after graduation. I spent the summer and fall at Bible camp and babysitting, and volunteering for anything the church needed to be done. Mom arranged for my twentieth birthday to be held at my good friend Elijah Marshall's house in town. It was a fully stereotypical Mexican affair complete with a piñata. After a few years of laughing off jokes from my church friends about being a "crazy Mexican" immigrant without a real job, it was nice to actually be celebrated with music and food and gifts.

As 2008 inched closer, Mom hadn't forgotten God's sign of the time to flee. She bought a little one-bedroom cabin about half an hour out of town down Highway 16 on Walcott Road toward Houston and moved everything out there. Like our Lake Kathlyn shack, she gave me the bedroom to set herself up in the living room, but I was gone in town so often already. She said she had always wanted me to do something called "individuate" away from her—which, if I remembered correctly, was Therapy Speak for leaving the nest—and my connections in town gave her a mix of proud concern.

So, she made a couple of important purchases for me: a 1974 Toyota Land Cruiser (even though I couldn't legally drive it, anything before 1978 was without a computer chip and guaranteed to still start if an electromagnetic pulse was sent out over the country) and my very first cellphone.

After a couple of winter months of driving me back and forth to my duties, an answer came in the form of an email from my former piano teacher Sharon: "If you ever need a place to crash in town overnight, I have an extra bedroom you can use."

Mom latched onto that right away. "I wonder if she would let you just sort of… start living there… until things get unsafe." She tasked me with replying and asking Sharon in another email. I felt awkward but it did sound appealing. I offered to do anything around the house that Sharon needed, seeing as I had very little money to actually pay rent. I had already been the regular babysitter for many of her grandchildren for a couple of years now; maybe that would help it come out in the wash.

In February of 2008, I moved into town as Sharon's new live-in housekeeper, studio cleaner, and what have you. I cherished my newfound freedom, and Mom felt confident we would still be able to "get the heck out of Dodge" when the time came.

Living at Sharon's brought independence but it was also a bit of boot camp. After twenty years of living with a woman who was pretty lax about doing chores whenever she felt like it, it was difficult to adapt to Sharon's life, which was scheduled down to the minute starting at 5:00 a.m. every day. She had been the epicentre of Smithers' cultural exposure for the past twenty years, and she'd done it all while raising three children by herself. She was happy to have me live with her, but I soon learned that I was expected to abide by "as long as you're under my roof" rules. She was tough love wrapped in leopard print and jazz; at first, it was hard to admit that I needed a bit of that.

Sharon's house was a duplex on Highway 16; years before, when I had been her student, she had only owned one half of it, and all of her instruments had been arranged in her living room like a game of musical Tetris. But now she owned both sides and every Thursday I would clean the house, saving the studio for Friday when she didn't teach. Depending on the time of year, I learned how to clean her car, clean gutters, rake leaves, shovel snow, take care of cats, run a dishwasher, and more. We still laugh about the day we learned I had been using fabric softener in my laundry for months, thinking it was laundry soap.

For someone without a "real job" I was certainly busy. At least once a week, I would sit with Sharon's mom, Linda Richmond, sending her dad, Pastor George, out for some fresh air. They had done everything together for over half a century, but Linda had suffered a stroke recently, and George was doing his best to care for her at home. He had a hard time leaving, but he always came home refreshed. I received great enjoyment from playing the piano and reading to Linda; it often lulled her to sleep, but I took the opposite of offense. For the first time ever, I had someone to call Grandma and Grandpa.

I spent Sundays almost entirely at church, starting with Sunday school, and then leading into morning worship where I regularly led from piano or played bass guitar, singing backup vocals. If I wasn't paying attention to the sermon, I was in the nursery or the Children's Church downstairs. It was never really a day of rest, but it was the doorway through which I saw everything else: friendship, potential romance, and spiritual connection.

Mondays, Tuesdays and Wednesdays during the day, I would go to the Creative Roots dance studio held on the top floor of a historical building that also housed the museum and art gallery. An air raid siren went off every day at noon, just so we knew it still worked, and the Bulkley Valley Farmers Market gathered in the parking lot every Saturday morning. I started frequenting the dance studio office as an unofficial receptionist in exchange for taking part in dance classes: Modern, Tap, and Musical Theatre. I was surprised when the owner, Dee, had agreed to the arrangement, but she and Sharon went way back. My classes were usually in the afternoon or evening on Wednesdays and Thursdays, so it worked out well.

On Tuesday evenings, Sharon and I would drive to the high school's music room to meet everyone who was part of the Local Vocals choir. Sharon and her friend Gail had been running it for a few years now, and I was excited to join knowing that they often travelled around performing at various summer festivals. I was quite possibly the youngest person in the choir, which meant I learned a lot of classics and standards—even more than I'd learned from Doogie in school choir the year before! I was delighted.

Thursday mornings started early with Coffee Break at the church on the hill. This was a ninety-minute time where tired moms could gather, send their kids to play with each other in a different room while someone entertained them (me), and then they could catch up, find support, maybe do a Women's Bible Study program together. Fellowship like this is what I pictured myself needing one day; the hope that I could be a wife and mother too increased with Apocalypse-free time. My involvement was an investment, a half-arc on a full-circle moment.

Thursday afternoons and Friday afternoons, Sharon didn't teach, so that was my chance to clean her music studio and her house to a hotel-level shine. And Saturdays were just for me.

She Works Hard for the Money (2009)

I knew I was lucky to live with Sharon rent-free, but I also knew it wasn't realistic to live that way forever even if I wanted to. Amidst all my other activities, I averaged about ten hours of babysitting a week, which equalled to roughly fifty dollars. I made do with hand-me-down clothes from friends, going to the Salvation Army for anything I couldn't live without. I walked to the grocery store at the other end of town once a week, and I made it my goal to get what I could for twenty dollars, or my four-bag limit for walking home, whichever came first. I lived on instant oatmeal, alternating apples and oranges, boxed macaroni and cheese, cans of soup, microwave dinners, and whatever Sharon said was in the fridge that needed to be eaten before it expired.

The best money I ever made was when I was "employed" by the motel across the highway from Sharon's house for a whole week. They said I did a great job, and they'd love to help me out if they could. I enjoyed turning the TV on to the music video channels, reliving some childhood memories of staying in a hotel with Mom while I worked. It felt satisfying to take a totally destroyed room and make it look fresh again.

Unfortunately, my lack of a social insurance card came back to bite me in the ass, as always. The motel owners said they wished they could keep me, but they didn't want to get in trouble. They gave me a couple hundred dollars cash and called it a write-off. I was disappointed but I understood.

I grew tired of living this way, with no prospects. The year was almost over and in my heart I didn't believe in Mom's prediction anymore. I didn't believe the apocalypse was coming anytime soon. I was especially tired of the one big secret: other than my GED, I didn't exist. And this fact, this secret, kept coming up, over and over, and getting in the way as I tried to forge ahead, making a life for myself that didn't anticipate the end of the world.

That week of working at the motel helped me decide for real that I was ready for the next big step toward change. I had already proved to myself I could do hard things. I graduated high school. I could find a way to get the documentation I needed to participate fully in the community in which I lived.

I already had my first cellphone, thanks to Mom, but I also got my first laptop. My friend Elijah had been going to the University of Northern British Columbia (UNBC) for about a year, and on one of his visits home, he brought a brand new laptop he'd won in a draw. Since he already had one, he kindly gave it to me. I started using it for two things: two-dollar DVD rentals from *Gone Hollywood*, and to research what it would take to make my existence here official without getting myself or my mom in trouble.

It seemed like my best bet would be something called "Permanent Residence Under Humanitarian/Compassionate Circumstances." It was a category for refugees, or people who couldn't return to their home country safely. I wasn't necessarily a refugee; I just didn't have much connection to the United States anymore, other than a couple of childhood friends, thanks to social media. The thought of starting over there was overwhelming. Thankfully, the paperwork had a section where you could tell your story and explain why you found yourself in this position—which is exactly where I could shine brightest.

The paperwork also required "community testimony" in which upstanding folks who knew me could write letters of recommendation about my character and how much I needed to not be deported.

Which meant I would need to tell people for the first time. Which meant I was about to rebel against my mom's wishes for maybe the third time ever.

My heart pounding, I scheduled a meeting with my pastor and Elijah's parents, the Marshalls. They were dual citizens from the States and had taken me under their wing to help in any way they could. I felt so ashamed, pouring out my soul in that office, confessing all the times I'd lied to them for my personal safety. But to my surprise, they surrounded me with support and love. They reassured me everything was going to be okay.

And then we got to work.

The first thing I needed to do was collect whatever forms of identification I did have. I had a social security card, and my graduation diploma.

Since the original was lost, I had to request a copy of my birth certificate. Thankfully, it could be mailed from the US government, and once it was, I protected it like priceless treasure.

The next step was getting a US passport, which would prove a little trickier. The only place I could apply for one was at the US embassy in Vancouver, and I had to be there physically. I could not drive or fly. But as word spread around the church of my situation, a young woman came to me and said that she was in the process of moving to Vancouver Island, and she'd be driving down with enough room for me to join. I'd just have to find somewhere to stay, as well as a way back up north after it was over.

That was enough for me. I went over to the Marshalls' house, and we began to brainstorm. Eventually we remembered that not only did we have mutual friends in Langley I could ask to stay with, but one of our church deacons also worked at the Smithers Airport. Maybe he could pull some strings for me to get a flight back.

Gratefully, the community stepped up across the province, and I was on track to go to Vancouver for the very first time. I decided it was time to let Mom in on my plan. It was already too late to ask permission, but there was still time for forgiveness, and I'd done it that way on purpose. I knew I'd back out otherwise.

The next time she was in town, she took me to lunch at Java's, one of our favourite places by the railroad tracks. It was always busy during this time, and I'd chosen it for that exact reason. I knew Mom was about to be deeply upset, but she wouldn't make a scene here.

I took a deep breath, trying to remember how I'd fought for myself a few years ago in Bella Coola.

"Mom, I can't live this way anymore. I'm going to turn twenty-one this year. I'm living on five dollars an hour, and I know you help sometimes—I'm so grateful—but you're running out of money too. This year is almost over, and nothing has happened, so I'm starting the paperwork to get my Permanent Residence."

She looked stunned. "I know 2008 hasn't gone as planned, but we talked about this, babe. No matter what God's plan is, going to the government is not going to end well for us!"

"I found a way, Mom. There's a special application where I can explain how I got here, and it's how they help refugees stay here. I think it's going to be okay."

Her face wrinkled in frustration. "They're going to ask you questions about me, Carly! They're gonna wanna know why I didn't do the paperwork a long time ago!"

I naïvely reassured her. "This is just for me, Mom. I'm gonna leave you out of it as much as possible. I'm going to the US embassy in Vancouver with a friend next week to apply for my passport, then I'll fly back and start the official paperwork."

"How did you get a flight?"

I paused. "Some people at the church are helping."

"So everyone knows about this."

"Not really. I just need a few people who've known me for a long time to vouch for me in the paperwork, that's all. I promise it's going to be okay."

She sighed and I waited, our plates of food sitting untouched.

"Well," she said finally, making a peace offering. "Just be safe and keep me posted."

"For sure," I said, smiling. Everything had to be fine. It just had to.

Being Twenty-Two (2009)

It had been a hard year for me. When 2008 ended, and with it any chance of my mom's prediction being correct, I struggled to figure out exactly what I wanted to do with that information. I didn't really want my mother to have been correct—I didn't want the world to end—but I also didn't want to question my faith. I kept shutting out a niggling thought at the back door of my brain:

If she wasn't right about this, what else wasn't she right about?

I knew if I started questioning her faith-based actions, it would incrementally lead to questioning the faith itself. I couldn't decide if the stress of pursuing my permanent residence documents was a welcome distraction from my crisis of faith, or not, but in some ways they felt one and the same. Either way, the common denominator cure for both ailments was my church community. Perhaps God was showing up for me now, showing up for me with the help from my friends.

I had no trouble being grateful for the help. It was only because of Elijah, his parents, my pastor, and my other friends through church that I was able to pursue the documents at all. Without them, the prospect of facing a trip to Vancouver and the US embassy would have been even more overwhelming. As it was, I had friendly faces to welcome me.

~

I had an interesting connection to the Lower Mainland despite only being there twice before—once for a History Maker conference in Langley when they stopped hosting them in Kamloops, and once for a Discovery Days weekend that was basically a recruitment retreat hosted by Summit Pacific Bible College. A friend named Melanie who lived there had been coming up to Smithers every summer to visit her large family of cousins who I babysat, and she'd said if I was ever in the neighbourhood to come visit. She attended Summit Pacific Bible College in Abbotsford when our youth group visited for Discovery Days, and I'd also run into her with her boyfriend, Steven, at a Starfield concert during History Maker, and I knew she was a sincere person.

I was gratified when I texted her that I was trying to get to the US embassy in downtown Vancouver and she immediately wanted to help. She said she'd talked to her parents and I could stay in her old room since she was staying in the college dorms. Her mom could help me get to my appointment at the embassy once I got to the city.

It was a whirlwind weekend that spring. On a Thursday at 4:00 a.m., I squished in with my friend and all her belongings and we drove for over twelve hours. Melanie's mom picked me up in a mall parking lot and took me to their house. On Friday morning, we got up early and hit the road downtown. About halfway there, I started to get extremely nervous. Booking my appointment had gone fine, but I was still unsure whether I had enough paperwork or information to qualify me for a passport. Looking up at the skyscrapers made me nauseated. Seeing all the struggling folks on Hastings Street hurt my heart, and I thought about how easily that could be me.

Melanie's mom was a rock through the whole process. She waited with me in the embassy the entire time, her warm brown eyes and calm demeanour an anchor for my frazzled nerves. She was a big city mom, so if there was nothing she seemed worried about, why should I?

My appointment was much simpler than I'd thought. I was surrounded by immigrant families who looked and spoke very differently from me, who came from infinitely more challenging stories than I did. Bouncing screaming babies on their hips, they remained calm, and so did the embassy workers in their booths. I could do this.

All I had to do was let them copy my birth certificate and social security number, fill out paperwork about where I was living now, and pay fifty dollars. A week's worth of babysitting if I hadn't been sent on my way with a little "love offering" from my church.

They stamped it and said, "Your passport will be mailed to you within eight weeks. Next!"

And on it went.

The next day, I was dropped off at YVR airport, and I got overwhelmed all over again. I had not flown since I was child, occasionally joining Mom on her Florida business trips. I wandered the halls, trying to find my gate and keep track of the only papers I had self-identification on. My connection at the Smithers Airport assured me he'd sent a picture of me to security and the gate so they'd know I was the right person, and I'd packed my school ID with a horrible photo on it just in case.

Apparently, I passed the test without blinking an eye, because less than two hours later, I was home. I took Monday off to sleep. Now all I could do was wait.

~

The spring and summer of 2009 was spent house-sitting. Sharon went away, her father went away, families I babysat for went away. I loved packing a bag and pretending I had my own home all by myself for a week or two. After seeing me walk to one of those homes in the dark on the Highway of Tears, some church friends named Tim and Elsa felt led by God to buy me a bike, and it was a lifesaver—possibly literally. I knew it was called the Highway of Tears for a reason, but I'd been walking because it had been my only option (I still couldn't legally drive the car Mom had bought me; it was starting to rust in her yard out on Walcott Road).

I had loved riding my bike as a kid, and I expected to feel the same freedom I used to, but after a few moments of riding, I had to stop as it felt like my blood was boiling from my head to my toes. I had to get off my new bike and bend over with my hands on my knees until the nausea passed. My coordination, while it had never been great, was getting worse, and I didn't know why.

Still, a bike made a good carrier for groceries while I walked, and I loved shopping, planning what I was going to make out of my meagre supplies and what was already in the kitchen at whichever house I was staying at. Nothing made me happier than inviting people over, making them food and drinks, and making them as comfortable as possible.

I dialled back on the "comfortable" after one particular night, however. Kass and a few other young women in the youth group ministry came over and taught me how to play strip poker. No limits.

Well, it turns out that we were all terrible at poker, but I was good at descending into a sweaty panic. My eyes were in a tug of war, watching and averting, watching and averting. Poker turned into dares to run out of the house naked, through the field to the river's edge, and run back. I felt like it was okay to watch that; I had to make sure my friends came back, right? They laughed and I blushed and they laughed at my blushing, mistaking it for propriety.

I tossed and turned the entire night after they left. I imagined the neighbours in the house all the way across the field had seen us and were going to tell the family who'd left me in charge. I couldn't get it out of my mind. Also, why had their bodies made me feel that way? Why had we played at all?

Never again. I had a future husband to remain true to, and a Heavenly Father I was putting all my trust in for survival. It was time once again to shove down feelings and questions that didn't line up with what I'd been taught. The Devil seemed trickier than he had when I was a kid playing Barbies with my friends. I was already praying that God would point that man out to me with a neon sign, because I hadn't the first clue who or what I wanted. All I knew is that I needed someone who stayed.

Maybe I no longer believed the world was going to end, but Hell after Death was still at stake. And who I chose to raise a family with was one of the highest stakes of all. If I worked hard and didn't waste my gifts and hung onto my faith, I would be rewarded in the end.

~

The year continued to feel hard. Not only was I under constant stress trying to secure all the documents about my permanent residence and under constant pressure with my odd jobs and my continued work with the youth group, I was also suffering the injustice of extremely necessary adult braces. After all the fear of what would happen if I got them and the world ended, after promising *not* to get them after they removed my tooth—Mom had decided that I was an adult now and she would pay to fix my smile. Dr. Kinkela had not been pleased, but he took care of me anyway. So did his dental hygienist, Sandy.

One day in June, I had another appointment to get my braces tightened. I wasn't looking forward to the low-grade headache and aching teeth

I knew to expect after such appointments, though I liked Sandy a lot. It had been a bad day all around: feelings of worthlessness, fear about everything in my future, wondering where the heck God lives sometimes, and an increasingly regular stomach pain I didn't understand.

I arrived at the office, resigned to my fate, and as soon as I was settled into that long, comfy pink "recliner" and Sandy left, tears began to seep out of my closed eyes. *Oh God, please don't let me have a breakdown in the DENTIST OFFICE.* But no matter how sternly I told myself to stop it, my tears came. A Kleenex box sat conveniently nearby (maybe breakdowns are more common than I thought), and I made fast use of it when Sandy came back in, hoping she didn't notice anything.

As she leaned over me, she quietly said, "I hope I'm not the cause of those tears. Are your teeth causing you misery?"

"Not today," I sniffed.

"Hmmm. Something else, then?" She smiled kindly.

"Sometimes," I replied.

She was quiet for a moment, then went to work on my teeth, saying, "I've been going through a real tough time lately too. All it takes is some commercial and I'm a bawling mess. If someone even mentions my dad, I'm a bawling mess. If my friend has something bad happen to her and she has no ability to cry, I'm a bawling mess." Then she asked me what colour elastics I wanted on my braces today, and I said I didn't care.

"Well, I have chosen blue," she said. "It reminds me of the sky and the ocean."

"It's a very soothing colour," I whispered through more tears.

We finished up, I stood, and then she gave me a water bottle "to replace all your leaking," and a ring with a cobalt blue stone in the middle that happened to perfectly fit my finger even though it was from the little kids' toy bin.

Sandy looked me in the eye. "Now go out there and get something just for you that will make you feel amazing. You deserve it."

"You hardly know me," I argued. "How do you know what I deserve?"

"I'm a very good judge of character," she said with a smile.

I walked out of the dentist office a completely different girl than the one who went in, my teeth hardly even hurting at all. I realized that I didn't happen to know (or really care) what she believed, because at that moment, she was Jesus in my life. She had her own problems to worry about, but she chose to lift me up and make me feel like a worthwhile person, something I couldn't do for myself. And now, on my finger sat a constant reminder of the Creator who made the sky that blue and the ocean that deep, and somehow loves me more than those.

What a way to remind me, in a place that normally brought me pain.

I decided that this was how I wanted to live. Not hiding from people or the future, but seeing a need and then doing something about it.

Mom and Dad (2010)

My life went on. I got my braces tightened. I cleaned for Sharon. I babysat. I went to my dance lessons. I sang in Local Vocals. I hung out with Elijah whenever he was home from university, and I hung out with Sharon's children and grandchildren—who were becoming like older siblings and cousins to me—whenever I could. I was now legal adult age, the world wasn't going to end, and I needed to make my life about *me*. It was not selfish—it was survival, independence, revolution. Do or die.

Or, at least, do or be deported.

I knew that once I started the paperwork, my life would be changed. I would have to tell the story of how I got into Canada (probably multiple times), pay money that I didn't have (definitely multiple times), and at the end of it all, there was no guarantee that they would let me stay. I might have to go back to the country I hadn't set foot in for over a decade.

But I had to try.

I brought the topic of my dad back to life, asking for his name and anyone related to him. Mom was reluctant, but even she had to admit I was old enough now. I sat on the information for a while. All I had were names, and I didn't necessarily know what to do with them. You can put a lot of fantastical expectations into a name, and my little-girl heart was picturing all kinds of heartwarming reunions... but what if all I actually got was the door slammed in my face?

I decided to start small, testing the familial waters with my toes. I would try to find my dad's other daughter, my half-sister Cindy Wilson, on Facebook. I prepared for a million and one Cindy Wilsons to pop up.

Only one name appeared. One. And it wasn't hers. *Cindy Parker.*

She was probably married by now, but still, it's not like *Wilson* was included in my results. This one name came completely out of left field. And then I saw her profile picture: three small children, mirror images of me when I was that age. I felt like I'd been punched in the gut. I knew beyond a shadow of a doubt, beyond Facebook search technicalities, that I'd found my sister.

I private-messaged her. *"Hi, my name is Carly Butler, and I'm looking for relatives in the States. I've been told that my father's name is Miles Wilson, and I wonder if you know him?"* I kept it pretty nonchalant, just in case.

Less than twelve hours later, I had a response: *"Hi. My father is also Miles Wilson, and I believe you are my half-sister. I wondered when this day would come. What have you been told about me?"*

I had no idea how loaded of a question this was, coming from her side of the story. For an unexpectedly short burst, I was on cloud nine, revelling in the joy that I had found my sister at last. I was like a child at the fairgrounds for the first time, wide-eyed and wondrous, having no idea that I was about to puke on the pavement.

With sparkly eyes, I typed furiously: *"I mean, not much, just that my dad and my mom were close friends, and mom really wanted a baby, so she asked dad to try to give her one. They knew it would be wrong, but they decided to try it one time, and luckily, it worked. And then we moved away when I was really little so I never actually got to meet any of you. I'm so happy I found you!"*

There was silence on the other end for a while. I waited anxiously where I was house-sitting... playing with the dog, coming back to the computer. Channelling nervous energy into snack consumption, back to the computer. Completely alone with 10,000 of my thoughts rushing through me at once. *Where is she? Did I say something wrong? She's probably just eating lunch too. What if she hates me? She's a mom of three babies, she's busy, calm your shit. What if everything is about to change?*

Finally! A message. Cindy: *I know a very different story, and I'm hesitant to tell you because I don't want to hurt you or jeopardize our relationship so quickly.*

Me: *I want to know the truth. Please tell me whenever you can.*

~

An hour later, the crushing pressure that had been building inside my chest all morning spilled out in sobs and muffled curses. I was glad to be alone, although the dog I was looking after was concerned. As the pup licked my tears away, I felt like she was the only one I trusted in the world.

How could my mother have done this to me, to us? How could she have lied about this for twenty years *to my face*?

An affair. Of course it was. Nobody just "has a married guy friend who decided to give the gift of a baby to a desperate single woman."

You ignorant home-schooled hick.

It got worse. Oh, it got *worse.*

My dad had been a pastor, his wife the church office manager, his mistress the worship leader. For three years. Before I was even thought of.

When Mom got pregnant, she told everyone that she'd finally decided to go to the sperm bank because she had no close family left and she wasn't getting any younger. She only regretted that she'd chosen it after her mom passed away. The church, friends and family rejoiced with her.

Cindy had been ecstatic. My mom was basically "Auntie DJ" to her, and they would often go on lunch-and-movie dates. When I was born, Cindy doted on me, and babysat every chance she could—completely in the dark about who I really was.

Oh, but our dad. He knew. He probably looked out into his congregation every Sunday and saw his dimply, brown-eyed bastard smiling right back at him.

A little over a year later, his wife finally figured it out. Everything blew up, within his family, within his church—so my mom took off with me and little else. She'd been on the run ever since.

The more Cindy shared, the more pieces fell into place. All those years I never knew why we couldn't settle down, why we were always *moving*, why my mom never seemed to have time or desire to play with me as I grew bigger. I tried to put myself in my mother's shoes. She had been in love with him, and every time she looked at me, she was reminded of the face she would probably never see again.

~

I will admit that, at first, most of my anger was self-righteous. I was already sick and tired of hearing about pastors' infidelities, and now my parents were just another statistic, with seemingly no guilt—only owning up to their secret when they were caught.

But I realized something else: nobody is immune to loneliness or desperation or even rationalization when something feels so right it can't be wrong. Sure, we hold Christians to a higher standard and can be eager to kick them when they fall off the pedestal. But maybe they were never meant to be put on a pedestal in the first place.

Once my high horse became more of a pony, I only felt sadness and hurt for everyone who experienced the ripple effect. My sister had been fourteen when she learned of the betrayal of those closest to her; it changed her, sent her down a path that would do more harm than good. I was grateful to learn that she had been able to work through her (rightful) emotions and become the counsellor for young people that she is today.

I have a half-brother too, but Cindy seemed reluctant to talk about him, or anything else really. She understandably felt a strong loyalty to her mother, Rachel, whom Cindy felt had already endured enough. She was still married to my dad, and it seemed like they had moved on.

After I updated her on what my life situation was, Cindy and I decided to keep in touch through social media. I also decided two things on my own: I wouldn't talk to my mom yet, wouldn't tell her that I knew the truth. And I was going to keep searching for my dad on my own.

~

I knew I wanted to find my dad for more than one reason. I was curious, but also I was deep in the process of getting my permanent residence in Canada, and I was nervous that I might not actually be allowed to stay in this country anymore once all was said and done. I had to hope that this familial stranger would offer a safe place to land if I needed him.

During this season of "unemployment," I was quite the popular house-sitter, and I loved every minute. As an illegal immigrant who couldn't get a job or live on her own, it was the best way to have a place to live, food to eat, *and* make some extra cash on the side. Throw in some free wi-fi to help me locate my awkwardly obtained family members, with erasable browser histories—I was in, I was out, I was clean.

So, in the spring of 2010—about half a year after I first contacted my half-sister Cindy—I had the big beautiful house on the river all to myself again. But this time, instead of playing strip poker, I was googling and trying to figure out how to obtain information without being traced.

Miles Wilson. The State of California. Insurance. (I guess the whole pastor thing didn't pan out very well.) I located an insurance website that looked promising, but to be able to send any of the employees an email, I had to click on their name and then click on what kind of insurance claim I wanted to file. Otherwise, everything was locked up tight.

It took me a while to figure out a way around it, but once I did, I came away with an email address and a headshot.

I felt my breath catch. After two decades of wondering who I looked like, there could be no mistaking that the answer was this man.

His skin was tan with a strong nose and jaw, just like mine. His wide toothy smile made his dark eyes crinkle a bit, just like mine. He had mostly white hair now, but I could imagine him in the 1980s with a full head of nearly black hair, just like mine.

I tried to swallow back my emotion long enough to type. In my message, I kept the same unruffled, nonchalant stance I had taken when I'd first contacted my sister. *My name is Carly Butler and I'm looking for a man who knew my mom, DJ Butler, about twenty-five years ago. If you're the right one, please email me here.* And then I typed in the email account I'd made completely separate from my mom's simply for this purpose. After Elijah had helped me make a hotmail account years ago, Mom had been piggybacking off it to send her own messages because she was nervous about her name being anywhere on the internet. Making my own address felt deceitful, but I wasn't ready to share this with her yet.

I sent the message and then I tried to sleep. Didn't happen. Checked my email in the morning, and received the greatest surprise.

Oh! My darling daughter! We've found each other at long last! I have been searching and searching for you and your mother ever since you left, but your trail went cold in 1998. I thought you had perished. But God has answered my prayers! How are you? How is your mother? Tell me everything.

He was so well spoken, and clearly adored me. I fell in love. We spent six days emailing back and forth, spilling ourselves and lapping each other up, all the birthdays and Father's Days and Christmases we'd lost being recaptured. I was delirious. One friend said, "You got your Hollywood moment!" and I knew it was true.

And then our first phone conversation happened. His voice was like melted honey; I couldn't get enough of it. Sometimes, I would check my phone and find a voicemail from him, just because he wanted to say hi and I love you.

After a week, we knew we should probably tell our significant others—for me, that meant telling my mom, and for him that meant telling his wife. Mom was over the moon, the happiest I'd seen her in a long time. And Rachel, dad's wife, was fine with our contact under two conditions:

1.) that she be able to read any messages between myself and him if she wanted, and
2.) that there be absolutely no contact between my dad and my mom.

This seemed fair and understandable. I told Dad to let her know that I would abide by this fully. This was about me and my dad getting to know each other; I had no ulterior motives.

Another week of bliss went by. We had reached a nice rhythm of emails and phone calls, but never got around to Skype unfortunately. It would have been nice to see his face in real time, at least once.

All was becoming normal. And then my dad brought up my mom.

Dad: *How's your mother doing? Feel free to pass along my email address to her, so we can say hi.*

Me: *Dad, you know the conditions. I need to respect them. I'm sorry.*

Dad: *Don't be sorry, you're right. I'm the one who's sorry.*

~

A couple of days later, my mom asked, "So how are things going with your dad? You know, you can pass my email onto him, if you want. It would be nice to catch up." Again, I said no.

More lovely weeks went by, and they didn't mention each other to me again. I breathed a sigh of relief.

June of 2010 came around, and my mom wanted to go for lunch with me, so we went to Chatters, our favourite pizza joint. I could tell something was different about her, but I couldn't place my finger on it.

After we ordered our food, she said, "I have a surprise for you." Tears filled her eyes and she smiled. "I'm in love."

That's what it was! She looked lighter and happier, and even had a bit of makeup on. I had never seen her in love before, and now she had transformed into a giddy teenager right before my eyes. It was foreign and strange, but I was genuinely happy for her.

Wait.

Oh no. No no no no.... "What did you do?"

I'm in love. What did you do? Great start to the lunch conversation.

Mom explained, "Now I know you said you wouldn't talk to him for me, but I went ahead and tried to find him myself. Miracle of miracles, I did! And it turns out that..." her voice started breaking, "...your dad still loves me and wants to be with me! I still can't believe it, I'm just so thankful. So, he's going to come to Canada and marry me. We're going to be a family again! And... I was hoping... you could help me shop for some nice clothes?"

For a moment, in that pizza restaurant, I floated into an alternate universe where I was thrilled that my mom was finally happy and cared for, and *wanted* me to take her *shopping*. Double-edged euphoria.

"When did this happen?" I asked.

"About six weeks ago. Oh gosh, Carly, you know how terrible I am at keeping secrets, so I'm quite proud of myself for keeping it *that* long!"

A waitress brought our pizza, but I let it get cold as I did the math in my head.

Six weeks... Dad and I had found each other eight weeks ago... which means that right after I had told them I was going to respect Rachel's boundaries, they went behind my back and broke them anyway.

"So?" she said. "I know it'll take some getting used to, but what do you think?"

"Uhmmm... well, what's happening with Rachel? Does she know what's going on?"

"Your daddy's still trying to figure that out. She's a piece of work, keeps threatening to—" she looked around and whispered, "hurt herself whenever he asks for a divorce. His current idea is to fake his death, and then disappear up here. Of course, that would be drastic, but it might be his only way."

I'd heard enough. I managed to squeeze out that I was not okay with this, and then I left the restaurant. I went back to Sharon's and cancelled every single commitment I had, from babysitting to singing in choir, and I just did not care. My Show Up No Matter What was exhausted, and I left. I asked some out-of-town friends if I could stay with them indefinitely. They welcomed me with open arms.

It was a small paradise. Their house was situated high on a hill overlooking rolling fields, a pond, and the mountains. They gave me permission to sequester myself in a bedroom all day or roam the hills and scream into the wind if I wanted. I blasted angry music, which I'd always disliked, in my ears constantly. I started long-distance dating one of Elijah's friends at university, a guy named Jake. I ignored every single damn email my parents sent me, no matter how much they begged for confirmation that I was okay. I needed to go a little crazy, so I did.

In those days of seclusion, I was scared. Scared of how far the cliff of my feelings was willing to reach before it dropped off into the unknown.

Anger and betrayal, obviously. This relationship was supposed to be about me and my dad; my mom usurped it and he *let* her. And then they made it about love and redemption.

At the expense of my broken heart and shattered trust, and secrecy from his wife. Again.

Guilt. Replacement. Confusion. Fear. Anxiety. Worthlessness. They all took their turn in the spin cycle of my brain.

I wish I'd gotten drunk *just once* so that I could call my parents and tell them exactly how I felt about each of them. Sober and numb, my honesty was locked up tight for the sake of being nice and sweet, like I'd always been. Even in the face of all their lies and cover-ups, Little Carly still wanted, more than anything, for her parents to be happy and proud of her.

The worst day came when I could finally form a coherent thought about someone other than myself: *I have to tell my sister.*

I finally read all their frantic emails, my heart sinking further. What I read could only be described as a roller coaster. Up and down and up again. *Dad is coming here. But maybe not. It's complicated. But he's definitely coming to be with us.* And over again. The left hand did not know what the right hand was doing, daily. But they were so in love, and according to the Jewish laws recorded in the Bible (Mom! We're still not Jewish!), Dad was more than blessedly allowed to leave his wife behind for us.

However, thinking about faking his own death had been a low point (yeah, no shit) and he wouldn't do it (there is still a God).

He was desperate. He had always considered us his real family; he was only really alive when we came into his life.

God, what fatherless little girl doesn't want to hear that?

Of course, I left those last parts out when I talked to Cindy. Even so, she was defensive and hurt, asking me every little thing I'd said and done in this situation, to verify my innocence. She may have believed me, but in the balancing act of her family, her work, and keeping her mom completely in the dark about what was occurring—contact with me became almost non-existent.

Another ripple, another loss.

Less than three weeks later, I came back into town. I showed up for my public dance recital, and so did my mom. I was prepared for neither of those things.

We made painfully awkward small talk over lunch; I filled the conversation with worthless gushing about my new (and first) boyfriend. I felt sick when she gushed about us being in love at the same time.

And so, just like my mother before me, I went where the wind whisked me. I decided to move away from Smithers, on my own, for the very first time.

Part Three

Prince George (2010)

In the early summer of 2010, and the aftermath of my parents' affair, I was ready to leave the security of Sharon's home in Smithers and made plans to try Prince George.

Many of my friends were going to university there now, including the young man I was dating long distance. Jake was in his third year and had plans to leave for the mission field in Africa as soon as he graduated and got married. For a few months, that plan was a welcome distraction, and when a Smithers friend offered to be roommates with me in a Prince George basement, I jumped at the chance. I didn't have a work permit yet but the immigration centre in the city would make it a lot easier for me to access.

Even though the relationship between Kass and me had slowly been fading away for a while due to her ability to work and date and travel, I know she was upset when I shared that I was moving. I thought she'd be proud of me, following a boy, but it didn't seem to matter. It was the final nail in the coffin of our friendship, and I mourned that our paths had diverged so widely. Learning that some connections are only as strong as their city limits was a hard lesson.

Sharon and Calvin and Michelle helped make sure I was ready. I knew they were excited and sad and a little worried. But, like family, they had a plan. For the two and a half years I had lived with Sharon, she had been making monthly deposits into a bank account I would not have access to until I left. Converting the account into my name and receiving a debit card with a *chip* in it felt absolutely surreal. Growing up I'd believed this was one step away from the government putting a chip in your head or tattooing your forehead with the Mark of the Beast (666).

I bought my first bag of groceries without cash and almost giggled when the earth did not open up and swallow me. *Insert. PIN number. Is that it?*

I left Smithers with a braces-free mouth (complete with a new implant to replace my stolen tooth), three boxes, a suitcase, $7,000, and eternal gratitude in my heart.

~

Prince George is a few hours' drive from Smithers, and while it is technically a city, it's far less overwhelming to me than Vancouver. It sits in a bowl-like valley that remembers the Lheidli T'enneh First Nations, and the Nechako River flows all through it.

The University of Northern British Columbia (UNBC) sits at the top of the bowl, and the migration of students from everywhere northwest of Prince George is large especially if you're seeking education outside of church ministry (you go to the Fraser Valley schools, also known as BC's Bible Belt, for that). It's an impressive campus, and I got lost a few times. I was most intrigued by the corner room that held "Interfaith" gatherings and chaplains. Any and all denominations represented by people of faith were welcome—including openly queer people and even atheists. I felt shock mixed with forbidden-feeling excitement that such a thing could exist in the first place. Every colour, culture, and bit of knowledge was found here; it made everywhere else I'd been seem a little boring.

My new boyfriend, Jake, visited there sometimes, but I think he felt safer staying strictly Baptist. I might have wanted to explore my options a little bit more, but Jake was already expecting me to be a partner in all his plans. Just on the other side of the hill from the university was College Heights Baptist Church, and I started attending with him immediately. They were a large enough congregation to have two services every morning, and that seemed like a lot of work to me. But I knew a lot of the same music, and it wasn't long before I started joining the worship ministry team.

Every Labour Day weekend before school starts, UNBC hosts a large backyard barbeque for everyone to attend, followed by an outdoor concert that is usually pretty legitimate. That year, the band was Bedouin Soundclash, and I was pumped. I only knew one song from the radio, but this was my first concert that wasn't Hillsong or MercyMe. I sang at the top of my lungs, and made a lot of new friends.

It was all a little off-putting to Jake. He'd been attending UNBC for a couple of years already, so he was used to the fanfare but didn't participate. I don't know how he had homework before the year even started, but he said he enjoyed it more than music—which should have been more than enough for me right away. But I'd moved here for him; I might as well see if there was something else to stay for.

~

My friend Missie had found a basement suite on Foote Street—which was close to everything—for $525 a month. Split between the two of us, it was extremely affordable—although I had no way of working yet and was keeping an eye like a hawk on the limited finances in my brand new bank account. Thankfully, our landlord, June, was an older woman who had already furnished our basement, time-capsuled in the 1970s though it was.

Since Missie was extremely busy trying to become an early childhood educator, I took it upon myself to be the stay-at-home roommate. I learned bus schedules, found the grocery store close enough to bring everything back on the bus, and then I cooked as much as I could for us. It was a challenge with only a two-burner hot plate and a countertop oven only slightly bigger than a microwave, but I made it work.

I was still getting my bearings when I saw some welcome faces from home. Sharon, her daughters Michelle and Vee, her sister Mame, and her granddaughters Delaney, Avery and Camryn. At least once a year, they did a "girls' weekend" in Prince George to shop and eat and maybe do a slot machine or two. It was always a recipe for fun, and I tagged along to Value Village to see if anything caught my eye.

It started out as a joke, but the girls found me in the wedding dress section and made me try one on. "You have a boyfriend now, after all!" they teased.

Laughing, I took the dress into the change room, even though I already knew deep down that Jake was not meant to be my husband. I emerged from the change room to gasps.

"Really?" I said, turning around to face the mirror.

Yeah. Really. I almost didn't believe it was me. The not-quite-spaghetti straps and bodice were fitted and adorned with intricate lace and beads designed into delicate flowers, before flowing out into a billowing skirt that had layers of pinned and tucked fabric to look like a cascading waterfall.

"You're getting that," they all said.

I checked the price tag. $150. Obviously, it was a steal, but it still felt like too much to spend, especially when I had no fiancé and little closet space.

"Don't look at the price tag," Michelle said. "Do you love this? Would you like to get married in this one day, to whomever?"

I nodded.

"Then it's settled," she said, and every single one of those gals started digging around in their purses. I started giggling and crying, trying to do the math in my head and not feeling quite as guilty.

One day, I thought. *One day, I'll wear that and then I'll be the one who has enough to be so generous to someone else.*

Breaking Up (2010)

I had just celebrated my twenty-third birthday with my boyfriend, Jake, and my new friends from the university when I unexpectedly got an email from my dad, who said he was unwell. My mom confirmed this, telling me that my dad's kidneys were in diabetic failure. He was in the hospital after collapsing and needed me to pray for him.

The roller coaster I thought was over started again, guilt being in the first two-seater car. I suddenly loved my dad more than anything, and I fell to my knees on his behalf. *I didn't want to lose him now. Not after all of this.*

A couple of days went by, and I didn't hear from either of them. I decided to ask Cindy.

Instead, she told me that Dad was fine. He had diabetes, sure, but it was manageable. He hadn't collapsed, he wasn't in the hospital.

And that's when I realized that I was the third corner of a triangle I no longer wanted to be in. I promised Mom and Dad that I would stay in contact with both of them casually, but I would refuse to talk to them about each other and what step they were going to take next in their grand love affair.

~

A couple of weeks later, I got a phone call from the local immigration office. Up until this point, I had been having mostly phone appointments, and one sit-down appointment with an official in Smithers to make sure that my paperwork was ready to send. The vibe in the Prince George office was very different; no one knew me here, and the stiffness made me feel a bit like a criminal as I was asked to recount my story again to a man who never stopped typing.

"So, tell me about your mom."

I swallowed hard. I made it so far trying to keep my promise to her, to keep her out of this process as much as possible. But I'd known the question would inevitably come; how could it not?

"How much time do you have?" I attempted to joke.

He stared, and I swallowed again.

"When I was a kid, everything she did seemed normal. Everyone in our church seemed normal, and Y2K seemed like a real threat. Yes, she brought me here and didn't do things the correct way, but I know now that she was afraid. She was doing what she truly thought was best to protect me as much as possible. The only thing she did wrong was her timing."

For the first time in an hour, the man let the mask fall, and he leaned forward. "Can I ask you... how are you... like this? You've been through so much, but you're so happy. If I were you, I'd be pretty depressed."

I took a deep breath and thought about how to answer in a way that didn't feel preachy. "I have my moments," I said. "The whole reason I started this process was because all I could see in my future was a dark room with no key if I didn't try. But I can truly say that I'm only here and doing as well as I am because God put some angels in my path. They got me this far, and I hope I can pay it forward someday." I swallowed back tears.

He sat back in his chair. "Wow," he said, and then just like that, the mask went back up. He continued typing, printed out a piece of paper, and stamped it. "This is your work permit. Use the information on it to fill out job applications. Don't lose it. You will start paying taxes. Good luck."

I made it out of the office before I burst into tears.

~

Now that I had the possibility of a job, I knew that I wanted to pursue it, and most importantly, I knew I wanted to stay in Canada. I couldn't let Jake have his expectations of marriage and Africa any longer, so one rainy day in November, I took a bus up to the university. I knew he'd be there, and I knew he wouldn't take it well. So, like I had with my mom in order to leave Bella Coola, I played the God card.

We were tucked into a little alcove where Jake was studying, and I said, "I've been praying about it a lot, and I just don't believe God is leading me to Africa right now. I'm really sorry."

We'd only been seeing each other for a few months, but he broke down crying. "I really thought you were the one."

I put my hand on his shoulder. "But now you're free to find the one. I'm sure right now, she's praying for a good, godly husband to take her to Africa. You'll be okay."

He sniffed. "Well, can I have one last kiss to remember you by?"

I really didn't want to, but I had just broken his heart after all.

Our last kiss, like all the others, was wet and left me feeling nothing.

~

The Pine Centre mall was a short bus ride or a twenty-minute walk from my house. I figured it was the best place to apply for work, because there were so many options who were constantly looking for help.

I cannot express how embarrassing it is to print out copies of a resume with "babysitting" and every bit of volunteer work I'd ever done when I'd just turned twenty-three years old.

I spent a whole weekend at the mall, and only got one call back for an interview—from New York Fries. The manager was about the same age as me, and he hired teenagers with less experience than me all the time.

I ended November successfully in my own place with a roommate, minus a boyfriend and plus my first real paying job. Things were looking up. I spent that winter making $9.25 an hour and trying to get the smell of sunflower oil out of my skin.

~

In January 2011, I took a bus home to Smithers. Sharon's mom and Grandpa George's wife, my Grandma Linda Richmond, had passed away, and I wanted to attend her funeral. I almost didn't make it because I was so nervous to ask for time off from work already. But Michelle said it wouldn't be the same without me, and I know I would have regretted it. The church was full of people and music; Linda was beloved. The service ended with all twenty-odd great-grandkids standing on stage and singing Linda's favourite song, "A Bushel and a Peck."

The applause was loud enough to reach Heaven, and I sat in the pew, stunned, a memory flooding back of my mom singing the same song. Only, she never sang beyond the first stanza, so I had assumed there were no more words.

... and a hug around the neck
And a barrel and a heap...
And I'm talking in my sleep about you...

Where my mom had planted questions and seeds, this family had grown answers and trees. And for some reason, all of them had chosen me.

~

Missie moved out of our basement to help a fellow student and single mom in her class pay her rent, and for once in my life, I wasn't worried. I could handle the $525 and take care of myself and enjoy outings with my friends. Even if nothing else progressed from here, it would be enough for me.

It was late spring when I got an email from my mom.

The immigration office in Prince George has notified me that I have three months to leave the country. I know you did your best and I trust the Lord has a plan. There's no way in hell I'm going back to the Lower 48, so I'm looking into Hyder, Alaska—which isn't far from here. No matter what happens, I'm proud of you and all you've done, babe.

What had I done?

Permanent Residence (2011)

After getting that email from my mom, I tried to keep myself busy. I spent the next couple of weeks hanging out with university friends and working any shift I could get at New York Fries, trying to keep my guilt and distress about her future from spilling over into my daily life. I was still waiting anxiously for news of my own future, hoping my permanent residence paperwork would go through. I prayed. I tried to have faith. But the silence from God and the government was getting to be a little unbearable.

It had been almost four years since I had finally confided in my pastor and my mentors that I was living in Canada undocumented. For so long, I simply did not exist, and there was the very likely possibility that if I made myself known I would be deported. I had spent so much time waiting to be condemned for my secrecy and lies, I never imagined that it would happen to my mom first.

Then, finally, I got a letter from the immigration offices saying that I had an appointment with the Prince George office at 10:30 a.m. on April 14, where they wanted to "finalize my application for Permanent Residence." It sounded positive, but I knew better than to get my hopes up. This could just be another bill I needed to pay so they could finish the next step, followed by more months of waiting. I told almost no one about this appointment out of that exact fear.

But I knew I would need someone with me regardless. On April 14, I took my friends Jenna and Allison downtown to the same immigration building I had been interviewed at months earlier. I had flashbacks of being rejected all over again, began to feel that familiar anxiety in my stomach that warned me I should brace myself for more limbo.

Jenna and Allison sat in the waiting room, and I followed a French-Canadian woman behind a closed door. We sat down at a huge conference table with huge conference chairs. She handed me a few papers and said, "Sign your name here, here and here, and you are a permanent resident."

What?

I almost blurted, "Excuse me?!" but instead I calmly said, "Really? Already?"

She smiled and said, "Yes! Today is your day! In a few minutes, you'll be able to celebrate with your friends."

As I signed my name, I could feel the emotion building behind my eyes. *This can't be real. There's got to be a catch I'm missing. Oh God, God, please let this be real.*

We shook hands, mine trembling; I grabbed my purse and left the room. I spotted Jenna and Allison sitting anxiously in the waiting room, and I debated. Should I smile right away? Or should I hold a stern face and then burst into a surprise?

It was no use; my expression disintegrated and I promptly melted into tears.

"It's all done! I'm a permanent resident! You're stuck with me now!"

We all started screaming and jumping and group-hugging, to the point where a receptionist urged us to quiet down. I felt bad but only for a moment. This day, which had cost me so much, deserved to be celebrated.

By the evening, the news had spread and my friends had thrown together a Canadian-themed party. Everything was red and white, and we played games and raised toasts. That night, I slept better than I had in years.

My only question left was: *What now?*

The Drive to Work (2011)

Now that the weight of potential deportation had been lifted from my shoulders, my urgency to catch up to my peers took its place. I was approaching twenty-four, and I figured that I was approximately eight years behind all the other twenty-three-year-olds as far as real-world experience, education and finances go.

The most pressing matter in my mind was employment. By April of 2011, I'd already had a valid work permit for a few months, and I'd been trying to keep up with the fast-paced environment of a New York Fries in the Pine Centre mall food court. But I felt torn between staying there and finding something I was actually passionate about, even if I wasn't sure what that was yet.

I had so much to prove to all my friends and family back home in Smithers. They had done everything to help me get here, and there was no way I was going to run back to them with my tail tucked between my legs just because life had gotten a little busier.

It wasn't long before I became stressed-the-fuck-out. I didn't realize how much of a support system I was leaving behind in my mom, my church, my people. Turns out, a lifetime of being home-schooled, trained to survive the end of the world and/or get married, fulfilling basic human needs out of thin air and others' kindness, Children's Church ministry, and acing graduation with flying colours had not prepared me for the real (read: capitalist with a splash of Canadian democratic socialism) world.

The geographical ability to walk everywhere with ease, and the unreliable but flexible life of babysitting and house-cleaning got traded for strict mall poutine shop shifts and memorizing bus schedules. I was often running late, in dirty clothes, eating poorly on the go, waiting for a late bus, or running through the deep snow to just miss an early bus. I was exhausted and frustrated and ashamed of myself. This was what I'd wanted for so long; it was time to buck up and be grateful. I was making over nine dollars an hour now, after all. It was time to invest in my university friends and church music and surely my writing too, why not?

I was absolutely determined to outrun the stereotype I'd been hearing for years—that I was a chubby, under-the-table-working Mexican-American immigrant who was also somehow lazy at the same time—and I was running on fumes. But every time I wrote on my blog, I made sure I ended it on a positive note, that I was doing okay—or if I wasn't, that I used language that spoke of God and my prayer life and my spiritual growth favourably; I was no heretic. Hard times were for becoming a better believer. Surely, Jesus was watching and moulding and teaching and shaping; even when I felt absolutely alone, he was still there, even when I was mad at him. Surely, my anger at myself and how terrible I seemed to be at life and at others who didn't seem to understand what I was going through was a sign that I needed to surrender to the Holy Spirit more. Surely, things would become easier if I prayed for my boss and invited my co-workers to church and started reading the Bible at the beginning *and* the end of every day. Surely, everything going wrong was my fault.

The other most pressing matter was a driver's licence, which was strange for more than one reason: I didn't have a car, I'd known how to drive since I was eleven years old, and the process was unlike American driver's licences in every way. My mom had sold everything on Walcott Road, including my rusted Toyota Land Cruiser, to prepare for what came next. So, when she showed up in Prince George out of the blue one day with an actual working Toyota Corolla as a last parting gift for me before she had to leave Canada (she made sure that I knew it was from 1994 so it would not be EMP-proof), shit became very real very quickly. But I was ready to stop being at the end of my rope due to walking or relying on the bus system, so I acquired some very different kinds of study books. Thank God for online practice tests.

In BC, if you are learning to drive, everyone knows it. The first stage requires a knowledge test at ICBC, and if you pass, you get your learner's licence, or your "L." They give you a red square magnet with a giant "L" on it to stick on the back of your car, which must be visible at all times. You must also have someone with a valid driver's licence in the car with you at all times. If twelve months pass by and all goes well, you take a driving test with an instructor, and if you pass, you upgrade to a green car magnet with a giant "N" on it for "novice." You may have other people in the car with you. Another two years pass, you take another driving test with an instructor, and then you can graduate to full licensure.

Most BC kids start this process at sixteen; I was on the track to be fully licenced at age twenty-seven, with sixteen years of driving experience but absolutely zero city road sense. I was... unexpected, especially to local police.

One early June evening when my mom was visiting, we decided to go out for dinner. Mom was grinning from the passenger seat, and I was paying attention to every single detail around me. Unfortunately, I was still learning the layout of downtown Prince George, and without notice, the street I was on turned into a one-way and I was going the wrong direction.

Like a scene from a movie, an RCMP officer also appeared out of nowhere and flashed his lights. I pulled over, my heart racing and face flushing. Did L drivers get their licences taken away for driving one-ways?

The officer was in his fifties and did the standard line of questioning. I showed him my licence, and then he walked around the car. Coming back to the window, he said, "Where is your L magnet?"

I got out of the car, and to my dismay, my magnet was gone—leaving behind a square shaped clean spot on my otherwise dusty car. "I'm so sorry, sir, it must have fallen off or someone took it—you can clearly see where it used to be!" My voice started rising with panic.

"Okay, I believe you. I'll just need to see your mother's licence."

"Oh, I don't have it," my mother said casually. My eyes bugged; three strikes, surely I was out.

"Why don't you have it," the officer asked sternly. "You're with a learner."

"It's at the house, I just didn't think I'd need it. I'm American, didn't realize. Sorry."

I knew it was frowned upon to cry when being pulled over to avoid getting a ticket, but I genuinely couldn't help it. I had worked so hard to get to this point, and my mom was being as nonchalant as the night we got pulled over in Bella Coola on my birthday.

My tears were interrupted by another car choosing to go down the one-way street the wrong way, and the officer left, saying "You got lucky this time. Drive safe."

As we drove away, Mom said, "They should really put up a sign about that one-way."

When we got home, I googled what my offenses could have cost me: $375, minimum. Almost the cost of my rent. Making it home felt even better than usual.

Deportation (2011)

Mom and I had one last lunch date together in the Prince George Pine Centre mall in July 2011. She was so proud of me working there and said the poutine I made was delicious.

She said that she'd considered going back to California briefly, and that was all the confirmation I needed that my dad was still somewhere in the picture. I was determined not to ask, and hearing her say she was going to try Hyder, Alaska, instead—which was less than an eight-hour drive away—was a great relief.

She had until the end of the day to cross the border and get her papers stamped. From there, she would have to stay in Hyder for at least a year before she'd be permitted to cross the border again. I was thankful that at least the internet was available so I could reach her; I was thankful that the government's consequences had not been worse. Hugging her while she cried and watching her drive away from me in the Pine Centre mall parking lot in a rickety old truck and camper was one of the hardest things I've ever had to do.

Why had God told her to bring us here if He knew it was going to end this way? Why did my possibility of a future have to come at such a great cost?

~

I lived in the Foote Street basement until the summer of 2011. The university semester was ending, and it meant a shift in who was continuing to be roommates, and who was moving on. After Jenna facilitated a meeting with all the young ladies at Eaglenest Crescent, we agreed that we got along well enough, and with great joy, I moved into a room the colour of a Tampax box.

We spent an idyllic summer doing themed dinner-and-movie-nights. We worked. We argued about whose turn it was to vacuum and wash the dishes, until we made a chore list schedule on a white board in the kitchen.

We did art projects and took small road trips. I wrote short stories about the "Princesses of Eaglenest Castle," which delighted everyone to no end. They were shoulders to cry on, and angels to depend on.

~

After months of silence, I received a strange email from my dad. It was late summer in 2011, and my mom had left the country exactly one month ago.

The other day, I got a care package from your mom sent to my work building. This is too dangerous. Can you please tell her I can't be in contact with her anymore? I'd really appreciate it.

Guilt got kicked out of the roller coaster seat by Anger, momentarily taking over.

Are you fucking kidding me? You started this twisted, toxic relationship with her again. You made her the happiest woman I've ever seen, for all the wrong reasons. And now you want me to BREAK UP with her FOR you? I don't think so. Here's the only contact information I have for her in Shithole-Middle-Of-Nowhere, Alaska. Now find some balls and tell her yourself. I don't ever want to hear from you again.

His only response?

I'm sorry I bothered you. I love you. I'll be here if you need me.

And Guilt was back in the passenger seat.

Was this it, was I really cutting him off for good now? Was he really going to break my mom's heart again? There was so much I still wanted to say. More than anything, I wanted to sit at his feet and say, "Tell me about my grandmother Eva," and I wanted him to say, "You have her eyes."

~

My very first job at the mall New York Fries ended nine months after it began. I had been physically overwhelmed trying to coordinate everything for a while, and in my failures, I reached my limit of the three-strike system and was let go.

At first, I felt nothing but shame. My first ever job in the real world, and now being fired from it after less than a year would be on my resume forever.

I decided to take this unexpected "vacation" as an opportunity.

Through social media, I had reconnected with a childhood church friend named Sirius. Their family had left Montana for Colorado about a year before Mom and I left Montana for BC, and we hadn't seen each other since.

Sirius was about to go through a painful divorce after being home-schooled their whole life and marrying extremely young, and they asked if I wanted to come for a visit. Now that I had a passport and a bit of money saved up, I got on an airplane and returned to the US for the first time in thirteen years. It felt like I landed in a recurring dream; it was familiar and foreign at the same time.

Our reunion was a little awkward at first; we had both been through so much separately, and we were not the kids that used to play in Sunday School. By the time my week-long visit ended, however, we had gotten our bearings again, and I returned to Prince George feeling confident that not only did I have the power to travel from country to country safely—but I had helped an old friend.

~

By the fall of 2011, I was ready to try being something new: a barista.

Starbucks seemed even more stressful and overwhelming than New York Fries, so I decided to try a brand new independent little coffee shop that had locations in a downtown café, a medical centre and the university. I enjoyed it very much, and it was at the age of twenty-four that I finally realized: I loved coffee. The smell of it brewing always brought me back to our wood stove in the woods, but not in a negative way. Waking up to that smell had always made me smile, and now liking the taste enough made me look forward to trying a new flavour the next time I was at work. Something about it made me feel like I was a real adult now, and I wanted that feeling to last.

One evening, I was closing up late for the long weekend at the medical centre, and while I was cashing out my till, the janitor almost locked me in. He noticed me at the last minute, but in that minute of panic, I'd already looked at my surroundings and determined how I would survive.

Three days before we opened again. I had at least that many days' worth of food and coffee. I could use my mop bucket as a toilet if I had to. I had a book to read and a jacket to sleep on. I was good.

It didn't matter that I had a phone and could easily be rescued. Like a spy in a sleeper cell, I had sensed danger and formed solutions and remained calm. Even though I hadn't lived in the woods for close to a decade.

I guess old habits die hard.

Steven (2012)

Three months into 2012, I was feeling pretty desperate. I was twenty-four, a barista for a company that was about to go out of business and I had no potential changes or exciting prospects on the horizon. I needed to get away. To rest, re-evaluate what I wanted from my life and figure out just how much of that I was responsible for reaching out and grabbing myself—and what should be left up to God.

So, I did two things.

I ran back to Smithers. It was four and a half hours away, but it would be my first road trip by myself. Calvin and Michelle Elliott were taking their family to Hawaii over spring break and asked me if I wanted to house-sit and watch their dog, Phoebe.

And I sent an email. It was a perfectly innocent little email, floating around in cyberspace and making its way to my friend Steven. We had been friends for almost three years already, thanks to our mutual connection, Melanie. They'd gotten engaged in Langley not long after I spent the Passport Weekend with her family; I even got a wedding invitation in the mail and booked time off work. But shock rippled through our friend group as the news spread that Melanie suddenly ended the engagement six weeks before the wedding. Not long after that, her new relationship with one of Steve's groomsmen became public.

I hadn't known what to say at the time, and I honestly wasn't sure if Steve would still want to be friends with me now that Melanie was out of the picture. But I started feeling an urge in my heart that I should say hi, just to see how he was doing. It had been almost a year since Melanie had broken off their engagement. I was curious about him.

I waited for a few days. And then this bomb fell via Facebook: "Melanie is engaged to Groomsman."

Poor Steven, I thought. I really should say hi to him now.

It went something like this: "Hey, Steven, just thought I'd say hi and see how you were doing lately, especially with Melanie's news today. Hope you're doing all right."

He replied quickly: "Hey, it's so good to hear from you! I have been doing great. I have so many good friends who have helped me through this tough season, and my job is really starting to pick up. I'm happy again. I haven't been in contact with Melanie for a long time, what's happened? I hope she's okay."

My face grew red. *Quiete la boca, estúpido.* Of course he didn't know. All social media connections would have ended long ago. So now, because I had to be *such* a good friend and check on Steven, I had the task of telling him.

Thank goodness I hold a self-appointed degree in writing kindly worded, diplomatic missives. He took the news well, and this exchange jump-started our conversation and new-found friendship. I spent two weeks in Smithers, soaking in the freedom, lack of schedule, mountain views and near-constant communication with Steve. Every day for two weeks, I would receive a good morning text that made me smile, and every night, he would say, "Let me know when you're home safely."

But I was determined to just be chill. No assuming, no jumping to conclusions, just friendship.

My devout new stance was quickly shaken when I not only got an email from him every day, but started getting at least ten notifications about him liking and commenting on a status, liking and commenting on a new picture, liking and commenting on a picture I put up ages ago... it was weird. Is this what flirting in the twenty-first century looked like?

After I got back to Prince George, it was time to get ready for Easter. Even though Jake was the one who brought me to College Heights Baptist Church initially, I had formed enough connections of my own to continue attending. Now, I was going to play Jesus's mother, Mary, in the Easter program. For some reason, Steve and I decided that Good Friday would be a great day to meet up again for the first time in over a year, and I made arrangements for him to spend the weekend at a friend's house.

He had to drive up eight hours from Langley first, and I was an anxious wreck the entire day. Sure, we'd already been friends for a while, but now it was different, and what if it wasn't real after all? What if it was just weird, and then we couldn't even be friends after that?

One thing at a time.

We met in the church parking lot, giggling nervously as we gave each other a hug.

Oh. You're cuter than I remember, I thought with relief. He was a grown man, and I was attracted to him, and we were about to spend the whole weekend together.

We decided to go for a walk, and I looped my arm through his. We had so many things in general to catch up on anyway, and we fell right back into the easy conversation we'd always had. But I felt butterflies now, which was certainly different, and a good sign to me.

~

We went to dinner, and then I had to come back to the church to prepare for our Good Friday service. Steve must be one of God's strongest soldiers because not only had he just driven all day to go on a first date with me, but he was meeting *everyone* in the church who had gotten to know me over the past two years. Over that weekend, he sat and watched me rehearse and perform that cantata no less than six times. That seemed like a good litmus test for everyone else in the building.

With our Good Friday performance in the bag, a group of us went to Denny's for a late-night breakfast. I could tell Steve was exhausted, but he managed to rally. It was close to midnight when we all departed into our cars, and Steve was about to head to my friend's where he was staying. I wasn't sure how to end the night, so I nervously got into my car and rolled down the window when he came over.

Please don't let our first kiss be in a Denny's parking lot.

He smiled, leaned in—and then at the last second, held up his hand for a high five. "Have a good night. I'll pick you up tomorrow."

Perfect.

~

On Saturday, we spent all of our spare time at West Lake. It was a windy April and not quite warm enough for the beach, but he brought blankets and a guitar and powered through.

I'd forgotten what a beautiful player and singer he was. We went through song after song, and I found myself naturally gravitating toward blending my voice with his in harmony. Maybe I was biased, but I thought we sounded lovely, and I wouldn't have minded doing it for the rest of the day—saving my voice for Mother Mary to be risked.

After sitting for an hour, I stood to stretch my legs and walked closer to the water. He came up behind me, wrapping a blanket around me with his arms, and for the first time in a while, I felt completely safe. I slowly turned myself around in the blanket to face him while still staying in his arms.

I'll be the first to admit that I didn't have much experience kissing, but I finally felt like I understood what fireworks meant. He was so tender and firm, I thought I might burst into flames.

That's how the rest of the weekend went: church, singing, kissing, church, singing, kissing. When he hugged me goodbye on Sunday afternoon, he whispered in my ear, "I think I'm falling in love with you."

~

From that weekend on, we never did anything halfway again. We started making immediate plans for me to meet his family and get a job in Langley, and for him to take a road trip to Smithers and Hyder to meet my adopted family… and my infamous mom.

Hyder (2012)

I know they say space is the final frontier, but I think it might actually be Hyder, Alaska. It is a tiny make-shift village at the very bottom of the Alaskan Panhandle consisting of about fifty to eighty people of differing family styles and, while it is technically part of the US, the only way to get to it is through British Columbia (unless you take a float plane from Ketchikan).

To get there, you leave Smithers and head northwest. When you get to Kitwanga Junction, you turn right and cross the Skeena River. Here the road turns into Stewart–Cassiar Highway, also known as Highway 37, and there is zero cell service for the next two hundred kilometres. Just thick trees and wild animals.

Once you reach Stewart and drive across the border into Hyder, you are in no man's land. There are no doctors, no police, no schools, no grocery stores. Almost no established society whatsoever—just a post office, a pub, a marina, a gift shop, a small library—and every ex-con or draft dodger who ever wanted to disappear amongst some very nice people who are live-off-the-grid types like my mom.

For years, tourists had flocked there every summer to experience Salmon Glacier, the grizzly feeding on the river, and getting "Hyderized"—a process in which you attend the pub and are challenged to drink a shot of 150-proof Everclear. If you sip it or puke it, you have to buy the whole bar a round. If you succeed in keeping it down, you'll be considered a fellow Hyderite.

By the time Steve and I made it up there, Mom had already been living in her camper for a year with her Karelian bear dogs. We had brought our own tent for sleeping outside, but after all the locals regaled us with stories of how the black bears had been particularly bold this summer, we squished ourselves into the camper gratefully. Three humans, three dogs, four days and no AC.

Over dinner on our first night there, Mom proceeded to tell Steven what she'd been telling me for the past twenty-odd years: that I was the lucky, beautiful blessing to come out of a one-night stand with her best friend. Steven smiled and nodded, knowing the truth, accepting Mom anyway, making me love him more. Part of me wonders if that just *is* her truth now.

I knew Steve must really love me when he not only suffered hundreds of mosquito bites (to the point of mild fever), but he got on very well with my mom. They had guitars, classic cars, and quirky senses of humour in common, and I often watched them in grateful silence.

For all its idiosyncrasies, Hyder is a physically beautiful place. The Nisga'a people and grizzly bears used to co-exist and share salmon; now only the grizzlies come back once a year. The mountains and rivers took our breath away as we walked everywhere, swatting mosquitoes and eating deep fried fish that was caught that morning and then cooked in a converted school bus. I was pleased to find out that when Robin Williams, Hilary Swank, and Al Pacino filmed *Insomnia* there, Robin had autographed one of the tables.

Our last day there, after we drove up a sketchy, gravelly road that reminded me of the Bella Coola Hill, we reached Salmon Glacier.

Even though we'd already talked about it a few times before, Steven got down on one knee and made our engagement official there, with the peaks, snow, alpine flowers, and my mother as a witness. She was so happy, and said that we should try to get married before Steven's birthday on December 21, 2012. The day the world was supposed to end, according to the Mayan calendar this time, instead of the Bible. We agreed to get married quickly, but only because we didn't see the point in wasting any more time or rent.

Mom took our picture to commemorate the moment, and then we drove back down the mountain. Five years later, we would go back and take a new picture in the same spot at the same time of year—and half of the glacier would be gone. I wondered if the world had been quietly ending in other ways.

But the day we got engaged? That day was nothing but joy. He was a Hutton, and I was a Butler; together, we were now the Buttons.

Wedding (2012)

On our way back home to Langley, we stopped in Smithers at Calvin and Michelle Elliott's house. Even if I still lived in town, their three girls were old enough to not need me as a babysitter anymore. Now I was a unique mix of friend and sister and daughter to the whole clan, and this home had become a landing place for so many of my moments.

I had told them and Steve about each other, but this trip was their first meeting. Wanting to make a good first impression, Steve grabbed his guitar, and I sat at the piano. As always, we blended together beautifully, and I could see emotion on my family's faces.

When we stopped playing, we looked at each other in the way that only new love can, and said, "We're getting married. Will you help us?"

And help they did. In nine weeks, we all planned a wedding that money could not have purchased.

By the time September of 2012 rolled around, Mom had taken a float plane back and forth to Ketchikan, Alaska, and succeeded at getting a four-day visa to come back into Canada for our wedding. The day before all of our out-of-town friends started arriving, she broke down crying and told me that she had ended things with Dad a few weeks before, and it had been the right thing to do, and she was so sorry.

I gave her my first full-bodied hug in a long time. "It's okay," I whispered through tears. "We'll always have each other."

For the first time since I was a child, I saw my mother go shopping for fancy clothes and jewellery, let her hair and makeup be done, to get ready to hang out with a large group of people for a party. I was so proud of her.

Sharon opened my old bedroom, truly her entire home, for my wedding party to stay in. Her youngest daughter, Vee, had married into a family farm with a private beach on Round Lake that we could use. The public Round Lake Hall was right next door and just big enough to hold the people who meant the most to us.

Calvin walked me down the aisle, hugging me with all his strength and guiding my hand to Steven's. Grandpa George Richmond stood in front of the lake and led us through traditional vows and Communion on an uncharacteristically sunny September day. When Steven dipped me for our kiss, Grandpa cackled and waved his hand at us as if to say, "you crazy kids." I wondered if he missed his wife, Linda, a little extra on days like today. I hoped his blessing on us meant at least sixty years of adventure were in store.

Friends travelled from far and wide, and with the Marshalls at the kitchen helm, everyone brought food to share. The Value Village dress my family had given me on a whim two years before came out of the closet, and my multi-talented friend Janet not only made alterations to it, but created a cake bejewelled with buttons and butterflies.

Steven and I sang a duet of "Set Me as a Seal" by Matt Maher, and then, surprising everyone except for me, Mom got out her guitar and sang "Unchained Melody" while I harmonized with her. We received a standing ovation and made my new husband cry.

As the exhilarating day came to a close, my feelings of love and community started to fade into anxiety and tension. I was almost twenty-five years old, and I had still never been able to use a tampon. Now I knew I was expected to get fully naked in front of a man, touch each other, be entered, make him happy. What if I couldn't do it, what if Steven had made a mistake?

We filled the entire back of his truck with wedding gifts, and drove twenty minutes away to the rustic bed and breakfast that had been booked for the night for us by family. We didn't say much on the drive there; we were exhausted and content to sit and soak in the silence. I didn't know how to share my virginal fears with him.

We arrived in our beautiful room, my hands trembling slightly as I tried to remove the dozens of bobby pins and flowers from my elaborately braided hair. I calmed slightly when Steven walked up behind me, put a hand on my arm, and said, "Can I help?"

Together, we unwrapped ourselves until we could breathe.

"What a day," he said. "How are you?"

I decided to go for honesty. "Exhausted and a little freaked out."

He smiled bashfully. "Yeah. I have an idea."

I made eye contact with him for the first time since we got there. How were they so crystal blue? "What's that?"

"How about we just go to bed? Like to sleep? We can try sexy things later."

I breathed a sigh of relief. "Thank you."

We slept for the next nine hours, curled around each other like fresh smoke through a newspaper.

~

My first thought when I woke up the next morning was: *I want a shower.* I was sticky with sweat from making vows out in the sun and dancing the night away. Plus, my new husband was a bit of a heater when he slept.

I must have been dazed the night before when I used the bathroom. I had been so elated to not have a billowing dress to avoid while peeing, I'd completely missed the giant clawfoot bathtub surrounded by genuine river rocks waiting for me in the corner.

I'm starting my day right here.

I heard Steven rustling around on the other side of the door.

With you.

I turned on the bathtub faucet and found some luxurious bubble bath soap in the cupboard. Then I took off the new lace nightie I'd been given at my bridal shower the night before our wedding, and I opened the door.

"Good morning."

He took me in, his eyes going wide. "Good morning to you."

"After yesterday, I need a bath. Wanna join me?"

"Absolutely."

For the next hour, we did nothing but sit in the bubbles and talk and laugh. Our wet legs slid against each other, and for the first time in weeks, I felt my whole body relax. Maybe this would be okay.

We rinsed the bubbles off in the shower together, unable to stop kissing. We didn't even make it back to the bed. Laying on the heated bathroom floor, he said, "You do whatever you want or need to do, or tell me what to do. You're in charge."

That was all I needed.

Our first time was gentle and awkward and perfect; not at all like that Barbie and Ken childhood game, or strip poker or movies or the primal femme dreams I'd had since I was a teenager.

That was a fantasy I was ready to leave behind for something real. I was relieved that I'd "made it"—I'd saved my virginity, and I had given it to a man like I was supposed to. And I enjoyed it.

I thought of Cowboy and every person since who had ever shown me attention so they could take something from me—and here was a man who simply wanted to give. Give me arms and a song and pleasure and food and a home and safety and a future. Even if the world did end as predicted in the next couple of months, by December 2012, it felt like more than enough.

Newlyweds (2012)

Later on that same day after our wedding, Steven and I met up with Mom and she surprised us by giving us her camper that she'd been living out of in Hyder for the past year. She said someone in the community had sold her another camper that she had big plans for. She hugged and kissed us, prayed and cried over us, and then she started rumbling down the road in her old truck; she wanted to make it back before it got dark and her four-day visa expired. I was so proud of her for being there to witness us, and then returning as she should.

One of the smartest investments we made for our wedding was hiring a decorator to not only set up the room into a magical wonderland, but also to come back the next day and take it all down. We were exhausted as it was and had enough to worry about—but now that we had the camper, we had more space to pack all our stuff, and we could save some money on our journey home.

We were three hours down the road and almost to Vanderhoof when Steve grabbed his tummy and said, "I don't feel well. We should stop at the first campsite we find."

We barely pulled into a parking spot and sat in the camper when he became violently ill, from front to back. I was able to find a plastic bag in time, but there was nothing to be done for his jeans. I built a campfire and burned them immediately, determined to tend to my new husband, thinking this was a one-off event.

We stayed in that RV park for three days and barely moved. At one point, I lost it crying, screeching that this must be my fault because we had had sex exactly one time, and I must have broken him. He laughed, despite the pain it caused his sore body, and he said, "This happens to me sometimes, don't worry. I'm allergic to a lot of things, but I highly doubt I'm allergic to you."

On day four of our honeymoon, Steve was feeling well enough to limp us the last hour to Prince George, where we took refuge in a friend's basement for a few days. By the time we had been married for one week, all was back to normal, and we continued driving, deciding to make a camping trip of it in Jasper, Alberta, before the snow landed. Finally making it back to Langley, we unpacked our presents, made thank-you lists, and started making our little coach house on Grade Crescent a coach home.

Two weeks later, I was in the emergency room clutching *my* side in agony. I truly thought I might be dying at barely twenty-five, but it was just a kidney infection that could be treated immediately. I didn't know that the lower half of my body actually had three holes, and now that I was sexually active, I was supposed to pee out of one of them immediately afterwards. It's one of many things that my upbringing had not taught me, and the nurses tried to hide a mixed look of shock and pity from their faces.

Sixty years of adventure off to a good start with one month of "in sickness and in health" being put to the test.

Soon after, we celebrated Steven's birthday, and we adopted an orange cat named Walter. Why not? The world hadn't ended—why should our plans?

~

For the first time in a very long time, I was eating three meals a day; at age twenty-five, my long-awaited curves were filling out. I resisted the urges to buy every necessity in bulk, especially if it was on sale. Now that I was successfully having penetrative sex, I figured that trying a tampon would finally be easy. It was not. I continued using maxi-pads, my new husband alarmed to learn that I was in the habit of wearing one for over six hours, layering toilet paper in to make it last longer. He assured me that this was not required—even unrecommended, and if I ran out, I would always be able to buy more. *Is this what security feels like?*

In June of 2013, we drove up to Smithers for a wedding, and I thought it might be time to show Steven my old home. Where I'd thought for so long that old ground would be my young grave.

We made the long drive out in our truck, my stomach turning. It had been over ten years. What would we find?

To my surprise, we discovered that the American, Ben, who bought it from us was still there, and had turned our Apocalypse place into a Buddhist meditation centre. Flags of every nation lined the road I used to ATV on, and all the wild brush had been cleared, cabins restored. His partner, Charissa, was long gone.

"This would be an absolutely beautiful place to grow up if you didn't have the threat of death hanging over your head," Steve commented, wrapping his arm around my shoulders a little tighter.

"Ben did all the work that we never could," I whispered.

~

As Ben gave us a tour of each cabin and barn, I was flooded with memories.

I remembered being so afraid that I could barely appreciate the raw beauty of the world around me. Remembered not being able to tell anyone why we were there, yet I so desperately wished that someone would ask me.

I remembered becoming a teenager, when this was all I knew and I believed that this was all I would ever know.

I had run all over these grasses and bushes, singing and dancing to my own little beat. I was prepared for my life to be over before it really began. I dreamt about my first kiss, feeling a tiny hand grasp my pinkie in trust, living a true blessed existence in a world of purpose. But they were supposed to be just dreams—dreams that the new millennium of economic collapse, war, famine, disease, death might not allow for.

All the worst things I could think of—that had been my future. After all, God had *told* my family it was coming, so it must be true, right? He was always right and true, and he had had enough of this sinful world. I remembered Jesus's Parable of the Ten Virgins. Five of them were prepared for God's return and kept their oil lamps burning all night long. Five of them were lazy, however, so they fell asleep. They let the oil in their lamps run out, and missed God's return. We were so afraid to miss God, we lit oil lamps in our hearts and our home here for years, waiting for the coming Judgement.

All I could do was hide here in this wilderness and pray that I would be counted worthy to escape, or at least be killed quickly.

I remembered how I played in these places, the friends I brought to life with my mind. The stories I would make up, not knowing yet that I was meant to write them.

Where I swam in the creek in my underwear because no one else was around except my mom. The long float, winding through the fields, all the way down to Willow Lake. No life jacket, just me and the water and the mosquitos.

I ran my hand over the decade-old inscription of "Carly M. Butler's SHELF ONLY" on the windowsill and felt the defiant satisfaction of being remembered. Ben had found it; he told me he kept it, even though he'd remodelled everything else, because it made him smile.

I remembered trying to go to sleep on the couch on December 31, 1999. I clutched my sleeping bag in fear as the clock ticked closer to midnight, waiting for the cosmic boom that would announce the end of the world. I remembered waking up the next morning, facing this, wondering if all the people I knew in town were now dead.

I remembered how time went on and nothing changed.

I remembered the day when I was fifteen and I was told that yes, it was time to leave. To go to the town. To have a chance at living, at growing, maybe even falling in love.

I took pictures with my phone as I walked everywhere. Pictures I'd never been able to take before.

After four years of wilderness, animals farmed and definitely unfarmed. Snow taller than my waist. Trekking every which way for survival whether by quad or snowmobile or foot. Storing up food that was never eaten except by kleptomaniac squirrels. Watching my mom break down and cry after the windmill for electricity died, and again when the pipes froze so we had to melt buckets of snow-water and use an outhouse, and again when our favourite dog got into the anti-freeze and seizured her way into a yellow-tongued death.

Four years of wanting to cry and ask, "Why are we doing this? Why is this happening to us?" but never doing it, because in the big picture, none of this mattered. All I could do was let go of anything that felt like emotional attachment; it was too painful. Too risky. And yet, even after all that practise at letting go, I still couldn't quite shake this place after I left.

I told Ben that the woods had become a part of me, burrowed into my bones, and even though I was free, I still wasn't. Fear still had a stranglehold, the wilderness still possessed my dreams. And I didn't realize it because, for a little while, I'd had another battle to fight.

The war I'd been waiting for never came, but as it turns out, the government cares about those who disappear into the woods, without any legal papers or intentions. So, I gathered up my intentions, paid and struggled and told and re-told the story for those papers. Three years, and now they were sitting in my file cabinet. I possessed so much more than a windowsill now.

When we finished the tour of the doomsday-hideout-turned-meditation-retreat, I said, "Thank you for taking a place that was a source of strife for me, and turning it into a sanctuary for so many others."

Ben smiled and Steven squeezed my hand.

As we drove back down the gravel road toward our future, I let the oil lamp I'd kept burning inside my heart all these years—just in case—start to burn out.

Part Four

My Body Keeps a Score (2013–2014)

After our trip to Smithers, Steven and I returned back to our life in Langley, where he continued his floor-laying work, and I continued looking for work of my own. I got a summer job working at Driediger Berry Farm, and I impulsively enrolled myself into a weekend-long birth doula certification class. Mom and I'd always admired midwives and thought having knowledge like that would be beneficial in an End Times future. I'd fully let go of Mom's predictions by that point (especially after the Mayan calendar went past 2012 with no problem) but I thought I'd still like to be involved in midwifery, remembering my puppy delivery days with fondness. I swiftly changed my mind when I saw the high school level course requirements and length of time. Instead, I was thrilled to discover that being a doula was just as important of a service and much more accessible.

I spent a weekend on a college campus expanding my brain and my heart until I was exhausted. I learned massage techniques and pressure points to keep contractions consistent; I learned how to listen and encourage and not chew gum in a birthing parent's face. I learned that this was a passion I could pour myself into, regardless of the fact that I'd never been pregnant or given birth myself.

To officially be certified as a doula, I would need to attend three live births and then write an essay about each one.

My first birth parent laboured for over two days. It stretched me beyond anything else ever had before, but seeing a new soul enter the world felt like seeing God. Steve picked me up at the hospital at three in the morning and I told him I felt like I could do that all over again tomorrow.

~

I booked my second doula client in May of 2014, due in July. I hoped I would be able to work around my berry farm schedule fairly easily, as the college students I worked with were always eager for more hours.

And then, a few weeks later, I found out that I was pregnant myself.

This wasn't planned, and it was a lot to add to my plate of essentially working two jobs, but it was unmistakably exciting and we felt ready.

My client Dani quickly became my friend Dani as she had suffered from extreme Hyperemesis Gravidarum the past seven months and I was beginning my own hormonal roller coaster.

I felt like a never-ending whirlwind of hunger, exhaustion, emotions both disastrous and euphoric. My pelvis hurt. My ribs ached. My *skin* was tingly. My poop was stuck. I, who had never needed sunscreen before in my life, now needed sunscreen if I was outside longer than half an hour. Like a basic white person. Zits were everywhere, more than I ever had as a teenager *combined.* Working at the berry farm felt miserable.

My brain became my enemy as its lifeblood started to travel to other places. I had forgotten to lock my car door, words to my favourite songs, the names of favourite actors. I entered the wrong PIN twice in a row. I nearly sliced my leg open because I was so desperate to eat the steak sitting on my lap in a tinfoil take-out box.

So far, I was able to laugh at everything I experienced. I'd always had a good sense of humour and also I had boobs for the first time in my life, a perk neither myself nor my husband were complaining about.

However, in the first week of July, some things started happening that were a little less exciting.

I started spotting blood in my underwear. Not much, but enough to cause my heart to race and my worry to get kicked into full gear. I called the 24/7 Public Health Line, and they asked me a multitude of questions about my health and what I was feeling, which I was gratefully able to say "no" to all. No cramping, no vomiting, no blood clots. No to many things I'd never even thought of.

They encouraged me to see a doctor within twelve hours, and if I soaked a pad or tampon within three hours, to head straight to the emergency room.

Four days later, I still hadn't even used one full pad. Every breath was a "thank you."

Since I was still doctor-less, I'd been going to a walk-in clinic at the local Superstore. The doctor was older, so it was weird to keep a straight face while he put his gloved hand up inside me. "You'll get used to this," he said. "Okay, relax your tummy."

I did.

"Wow, you've got really tight tummy muscles. Do you go to the gym?"

Nope, but I appreciate what you're trying to do.

"Everything looks okay and sealed up. It's not an ectopic pregnancy so that's good. I'm gonna send you over to book an ultrasound. Normally it would take weeks to book one, but I'm going to put "threatened miscarriage" on your chart *just* so that they schedule you in quicker, okay?"

I swallowed nervously. "Okay."

He smiled, and on his way out the door, said, "I'll see you in seven months." I clung to that like a prophecy.

I had two samples of blood taken, three days apart, so they could compare my hormone levels.

Apparently, if my pregnancy was being "maintained," then the HCG hormone would double every day.

The blood tells many stories, and I didn't know mine yet—except that my type was A positive, which I was told was very good to have, and I kept telling myself that I have A+ blood, so really there was nothing to worry about, right?

Later that week, I parked at Valley Imaging Clinic, ten minutes before I was supposed to check in for my ultrasound. I sat in my car. I waited, I listened to music, I cried. I had been bleeding off and on for five days now, and I was still waiting for my blood hormone results, and I just... I needed to know if my baby was okay. Every minute felt like an eternity.

I laid on the table in a dimly lit room, trying to just keep breathing, trying to keep the cushion from sliding out underneath my hips while the stone-faced tech ran a wand over my jellied belly. Searching, searching, searching....

She said I had a very full bladder. A little too full, perhaps. She told me to go empty it so that she could do a vaginal ultrasound. I was prepared for this possibility. I saw Jennifer Lopez's *The Back-up Plan*. Whatever would give me that heartbeat.

More cold gel... an aching probe... *this will be worth it, this will be worth it, this will be worth it....*

So why was everything so quiet?

"When's your estimated due date again?"

"February twentieth. I should be almost eight weeks now."

"You'll need to go back and confer with your doctor. What I'm seeing does not indicate eight weeks."

I tried to keep the tears back. "Okay? So… nothing's wrong, though? It could just be too early to get a heartbeat, right?"

"Just make sure you talk to your doctor. You can clean yourself up now."

It took seven minutes. To go in and come out. Really, though, it was seven years.

I sat in my car again, and decided to call the walk-in clinic, hoping they would have my blood hormone results.

"Your first test showed your hormones at around 13,000. Now they're over 18,000, so everything looks good. Dr. Aspinall will be in at 1:30 p.m. today if you'd like to talk to him."

I nearly cried again with relief. "Thank you. I'll be in at 1:30."

For the next two hours, I distracted myself with food and the superfluous lives of celebrities in magazines at the library. I gave a brief update on Facebook, then answered the flood of caring texts and comments.

I arrived at the walk-in clinic exactly at 1:30. The clinic was empty, and I rejoiced. When Dr. Aspinall heard that my blood hormones were still going up, he gave a double-fist pump. I officially loved him after that.

He had the ultrasound report faxed over (yes, faxed) and we looked at it together.

Not only had there not been a heartbeat, there hadn't even really been a *baby* to see. They base it by seeing what they call a "yolk sac" and "fetal pole," which is kind of a fancy term for the spine. Therefore, it could not be called a "viable fetus" yet. Either something was wrong, and I would miscarry—or it was simply too early to tell.

Dr. Aspinall gave me another requisition to take back to Valley so that I could book another ultrasound in a couple of weeks, as well as a form to have more blood taken later in the week.

It was four o'clock by the time I got home. Steve got home not long after that, and we collapsed into a hug for a while. The kind with no words, only touch and requited feeling.

Steve told me, "We'll keep trusting the blood and the size of your boobs. Cause, honey, those things are *still* growing."

~

Days passed. I stopped bleeding and started puking. Hope returned, and every time a wave of nausea washed over me, I smiled. *Baby Button is still here, and they want me to know it.*

A few days later, Steve and I went to the hospital for my very first Maternity Clinic appointment. All of my walk-in clinic and blood hormone and ultrasound info had been sent over to them; Dr. Hansen told me to get my blood hormone done again that day, and that he'd get me an ultrasound earlier than the thirty-first. It all sounded awesome to me.

Until.

"Can you call over to Valley and tell them to get us an ultrasound this week?" He asked the receptionist. "Chance of miscarriage is very high with her."

"Of course, Doctor. Okay, Carly, you now have an ultrasound on Wednesday. Take your blood test today and call us on Friday with all your results."

Something in me went numb after that.

I had my blood taken and was told I could check my online results that evening.

I went home and slept for three and a half hours. I didn't realize it then, but I was done. Giving up. Letting it get to me. I was back in the wilderness of my earlier years, the mindset of hoping for the best yet preparing for the worst. I forgot to trust the blood and the boobs like Steve told me to.

Even reading my results later didn't faze me. *Oh awesome, my hormones are up from 18,000 to over 28,000. Doesn't matter. I must have done something wrong; now it's over.*

~

That night, we lay in bed and talked. Well, more like I had a breakdown and Steve held me. Then we talked. I poured out all my fears, not even realizing that I was talking about this miscarriage as though it was a "when," not an "if."

What if I'm home alone when it happens? What if I can see our baby? What do you DO with a miscarried baby? I'm scared of the pain, but I'm even more scared of the After. I'm scared I'll just fall apart and never get out of bed again. You deserve more than that. I'm sorry. I'm sorry. I'm sorry. I want to be strong. I want to be brave. But holding it in makes me dissolve, and what if holding that stress in is bad for the baby? But what if letting it out like this is bad for the baby too? I'm sorry. I'm sorry. I'm sorry.

And then he cried, and spoke, and I was shaken out of my fearful stupor. "I'm not even *thinking* that way right now. Our baby is still growing in there, and I still believe in it! Do *you*? Whatever happens, you are loved and we *will* get through this together. You will *never* be a burden or a disappointment to me, got it?" He rubbed and kissed my belly over and over, whispering prayers into our child's unformed ears.

Tomorrow would be my next ultrasound. I felt like a broken record. But I still was not bleeding, and my hormones were still going up. I trusted that my Father had a plan that I would be able to walk in.

~

July 16, 2014, was one of the best and worst days of my life.

It started at one in the morning. My doula client and friend Dani called me to say that she'd been in active labour for a few hours now, and she'd like me to come to the house as soon as possible. Their family was planning an at-home water birth, so I safely raced to their house. I told them that if she was still labouring around noon, I would unfortunately need to leave for about an hour for my own ultrasound—but I would be back no matter what.

I needn't have worried. I witnessed a beautiful, healthy baby girl come out of the water and into her parents' arms by 9:30 a.m. I wasn't totally sure what I thought about good vibes or energy or juju, but certainly that couldn't be a bad way to start my day and go into my appointment.

Steve was there with me this time. We knew that this ultrasound would be the make-or-break-it, and he wanted to be there. He expected to be brought into the ultrasound room later to hear a heartbeat if there was one.

Instead, I left the clinic and took him outside with me. I waited until I reached the bottom of the stairs where I knew there was a bench we could sit on. And there, I told him.

There was no Baby Button. Technically, there never was. I experienced what is (terribly) called a "blighted ovum," which means that our fertilized egg never quite made it to the embryo stage. However, it stayed inside my uterus and formed a protective sac around it, as it would normally. This was enough to keep my blood hormones skyrocketing, my breasts growing, my heart hoping that everything was okay.

It was probably already over by the time I took that pregnancy test on Father's Day weekend.

I began to hate my body that day. Sure, it did its job and didn't keep a non-viable embryo growing. But to lie to me about it? To trick me for the past five weeks? That was bullshit.

Trust the hormones, the blood, we said. *Trust the growing boobs,* we said. Sure.

Now, I had to choose between surgery or take pills that would make my uterus cramp and contort like I was in labour.

Over the span of twenty-four hours (hopefully) I would most likely be doubled over in pain while my body expelled the tissue of a sac, a placenta and a defunct egg. And *then* I had to fucking collect it in a zip-lock bag or a Tupperware container or whatever and take it back to the hospital so they can examine it to make sure that nothing got left behind to try and infect me. Because as long as that godforsaken sac was there, my body would continue to believe that it was pregnant—and it would also prevent me from becoming pregnant *again*, should I try.

This changed everything. I was starting to buy maternity clothes and getting rid of old clothes I knew wouldn't fit me anymore. I had quit my job. I was writing a pregnancy diary. I shared my hopes and dreams with my husband, my friends and family.

And now, I didn't even want to see or talk to anyone. I just wanted to be alone and watch Netflix all day, with the comfort of knowing that my people were still there should I change my mind.

I was scared. I was still tired from attending the birth the previous night. Throughout the day, I roller coastered between staring numbness and unstoppable tears.

I still *felt* pregnant. That was the whole problem.

~

Steve was my broken-hearted rockstar of a man. He let me do whatever I wanted or needed to, while making sure I still ate and slept. Part of me wished he wouldn't, because then I could start wasting away to ghost level; then everyone could know how I felt inside.

He said he didn't realize how attached he was to Baby already, until that day. Neither did I, really.

Thankfully, every doctor and assistant at the Maternity Clinic in the hospital was like a grief counsellor. Calling it a loss, and not just telling us to get over it and move on. Encouraging us to do something together that will create closure for us.

I started thinking about getting a tattoo.

I took home a drug called Misoprostol. I'll never forget the doctor who gave the pills to me. She was a smaller, older woman—I figure she'd been a doctor for a long time, probably been the bearer of bad news for countless people.

Yet, she had tears in her eyes as she hugged us and tucked the envelope of pills into my hand because she knew we couldn't pay for them. Compassion.

~

I chose the drug out of fear and familiarity: I had never had surgery before, and I knew how to take pills.

Within half an hour of swallowing them, I vomited them and my sandwich into a bucket in the living room.

I grimaced when I realized the only other option left to me. I took the four remaining pills out of the envelope and awkwardly pushed each one inside my cervix, hoping that they wouldn't get lost somewhere. I never took Biology, and vaginas are so mysterious.

Steve held my other hand and kept his red-veined eyes on my face the entire time.

~

I didn't know if or when the pills would start to take effect, so I put a pad on, and we cuddled on the couch watching TV, petting the cat. Anything to ward off the thoughts of Death and the Unknown that were facing us. I felt foolish for thinking that leaving the woods meant that being a mother was in the cards for me.

We went to bed, and I felt okay. Maybe I'd done it wrong.

Hours later, I was awakened by the greatest pain I'd ever felt in my entire life. My whole body shook as I made a hunching crawl down the stairs to our bathroom. I felt like an atom that was about to split in half; I had no control.

For the next hour, the bathroom was my home. I kicked Steve out; I wanted to be alone. I didn't want him to see how I was being melted down in an offering to a cruel god that was only appeased by blood, sweat, tears, shit and vomit.

In a haze, I remembered the other pills. The Tylenol-3s. I reached out for them like a life raft, barely taking a moment to read the instructions. An eternity of twenty minutes passed, and finally I felt a tinge of sweet relief. I was able to gather the strength to take some toilet paper and reach down between my legs.

The pink tissue of my not-baby had to be collected and taken to the hospital for analysis. Something cold and hard and clinical came over me, and I stopped crying as I stared at the mass that had been propelled from me so violently.

Do what has to be done. This is tough, but you have to be tougher.

I put the pieces of myself into a pad and a zip-lock bag. Took a shower. Stared at my face in the mirror. There was nothing in my eyes. I had just ended my very wanted pregnancy. Shouldn't I be falling apart?

We'd been assured that the whole "process" would take twenty-four hours or less. My body continued to shake, rattle, roll and bleed out for three weeks.

After going to the same doctor in desperation, she welcomed and treated us even though we weren't technically her patients. After using a clamp bigger than my pelvis (Steve faithfully holding my hand without even a swoon), she found the source of the problem: the sac had gotten stuck, of all things, inside my cervix—causing my uterus to contract and bleed non-stop in attempts to get it out.

I wish I had chosen the surgery.

The hatred for my body continued. I grit curses in my teeth against it daily; first you can't hold onto a pregnancy, and now you can't get rid of it? Friendship over.

In the midst of all this, my best friend Sirius dropped everything in their life to come be with us for a weekend. Work, new partner, long flights—didn't matter. It was time for poutine, *Parks and Recreation*, laughing and crying about the shit of it all.

It was a beautiful weekend. There was no pressure on me to do anything, and the one thing I really wanted to do was have a memorial at the beach.

So we did. We found the perfect *Thinking of You* balloon, tied some love notes to it, and then waded out into the water to let it go. Sirius took photos for us, of us, that I still treasure to this day.

I watched and watched and watched that balloon sail away until I could watch no more. Sometimes I feel like I'm still watching, still waiting—but for what, I don't know.

After Sirius returned home, my life became a series of goodbyes.

Monday: deleting the pregnancy apps and resetting the Period Tracker app on my phone.

Tuesday: calling the local midwifery clinic and letting them know I would no longer be needing their services.

Wednesday: packing the maternity clothes and newborn onesies away.

Thursday–Sunday: getting lost in Netflix and my bed, trying to forgive ignorant people who said, "Well, you're young, you can always try again!"

Steve could no longer take any more time off work. His first day back, he came home, laid down on the living room rug and cried into the fibres. I laid next to him, all out of tears for the day.

I whispered to him that I would love it if we tried starting over in Smithers. He nodded, and we started making plans.

Starting Over (2014–2015)

The move back to Smithers felt slow and quick at the same time. I fled Langley the moment I confirmed with the Marshalls that I could stay in their basement while I started work at Starbucks three blocks away—almost exactly what I'd done a decade ago, after leaving Bella Coola in a helicopter.

Steve had stayed behind to pack up our place in Langley, but it didn't make much sense for him to drive anything up for fourteen hours before we even had somewhere to live. Coming up in early August, I'd almost missed the window of end-of-summer rentals being available. I was making phone calls and driving from rental to rental after each of my eight-hour shifts, the floor of my car littered with Starbucks cups. None of the rentals were quite right, or the landlords would choose someone else.

Finally, I caught a break. A mobile home out of town on an acreage, and it cost the same as what we'd been paying for a tiny converted garage in someone's city backyard. The previous renter had smoked inside a lot and it would be a bit of a commute to work, but it was so quiet here off the highway. There were trees and a pond, and a big yard with a little old barn. Space to recover and find ourselves again.

We started unpacking in early September, and celebrated our second wedding anniversary by being a musical part of the wedding of my dear friends' Elijah Marshall and former Prince George roomie Jenna. Even if it took a while for Steve to find work as a floor installer, I knew I could shoulder us for a while. He was enjoying resting with Walter the cat and tinkering in the barn. For the first time ever, we had a second bedroom to turn into a music room; we were starting to smile again.

Eighty-nine days after I'd started working at the Safeway Starbucks, I called Steve in tears: "I just got fired."

"Fuck," he said.

What else was there to say?

I wouldn't figure it out until much later, but Safeway Starbucks is a completely different establishment than solo Starbucks—and the Safeway manager was on a complete power trip. After getting fired from New York Fries after nine months, I thought I was a simpleton on a downward trend, and I just needed to try harder. I tried to make three drinks a minute like he asked (sometimes he would stand there and time me) but I was often there by myself with one working machine and a line out the door. My lifelong struggle to concentrate on keeping my limbs coordinated still plagued me; I worked myself so hard, I developed a pinched nerve in my back that made my arm go numb. Not even a doctor's note earned me a rest. Nothing could have made me good enough for that manager; his turnover was frequent, always letting new people go just before their ninety-day probation was up and they could join the Safeway union.

But it still stung. I felt guilt weighing down on me as my only justification for bringing us all the way up here on a whim disappeared. It was winter now, and moving back would be impossible even if we wanted to. I used the internet to look for work, but for the most part, we went into hibernation mode, living on Kraft dinner with hot dogs and saving gas as much as possible.

My lowest point was when my tooth implant from 2010 inexplicably shattered with no way of replacing it, and pretending I was already a paying customer at Tim Hortons so that I could ask for "two more butters"—which I took home to make our last box of macaroni and cheese.

We made an effort to show up for Christmas with Sharon and the Elliotts and the rest of the family; my mom came down from Hyder for a few days too. Just after New Year's Day 2015, Steve came down with an unexplained illness, burning up from fever and spots breaking out all over his body.

I drove him to the emergency room, knowing he had a laundry list of allergens to look out for and no EpiPen.

The doctor's eyes widened in shock when he saw Steve. "Is that... chicken pox?" he said incredulously.

Indeed it was. That was when I learned Steve had never had it as a child, and the vaccine for it had not been available until he was a teenager and it didn't seem necessary.

"There's not much you can really do except ride it out," the doctor said. "Lots of oatmeal baths and rest. It can become very serious in adults, so please come back if it continues to get worse."

Back into hibernation mode we went. For weeks, the only activity we did was make or take baths, and take out one DVD to put in another DVD. Steve thought he might be dying, and I ordered him not to.

By the end of January 2015, there was an end to the chicken pox. We'd heard there was a music night at the Art Gallery in town, and we signed up. We called ourselves Agent Button and we sang all the songs we'd been keeping to ourselves for the past two and a half years. People seemed to like our music, and this opened the door to doing coffee shops about once a month (leading us all the way up to performing in the Midsummer Festival amidst some really good Canadian bands). It certainly didn't pay the bills that were starting to pile up, but it gave us a new lease on hope—that spring and work and life would soon return.

And sure enough, that spring, a friend invited me out for coffee at Two Sisters Café, to tell me that she'd had to turn down a nanny job because she was too busy, but that she'd made a recommendation with my phone number, hoping I could take the job instead.

It turned out perfectly. Right away, I became the full-time nanny of three young children who lived right in town. The oldest were in school, so I was mainly in charge of the youngest most of the time. Then I'd drive their minivan to do school pickup and groceries; I always had dinner and homework sorted by the time their parents came home. I was also responsible for the family's mischievous golden retriever named Poppy. She was sweet, but had a temper after being mistreated by her last owner. My nanny family had adopted her with good intentions, but Poppy became a bit too unpredictable around young children. When they sent out a group text to everyone looking to re-home her, I replied as fast as I could that we'd love to take her. My childhood dreams of having a grumpy old golden retriever like Shadow from *Homeward Bound* were finally coming true. Poppy and Walter were our first children.

By the time summer rolled around, the hardships of our pregnancy loss, the long winter and our "fresh start" felt long behind us. My nanny family had taken on a café contract at the airport and promoted me to being their part-time nanny and part-time café manager. Steve had taken a temporary job as a shipper/receiver for the electric company in town, our little animal family was thriving at home, and we were just starting to re-join my childhood church in a music ministry capacity.

And then God did something none of us expected: He led the head pastor to move away. When we looked to the associate pastor (who had been my first youth pastor back in the early days, before Bella Coola and the ministry team split) to take over, he announced that while he and his family were going to stay in Smithers, they felt led to leave the church on the hill, to go into the community instead. To plan events, to love others, to see a need and fill a need, without any evangelistic implications. Anyone was welcome to join them.

The people were not happy. It was one thing if God called you to move to a different town, but leaving the physical building while staying in town? To help others who didn't even try coming to the church, without preaching to them? To invite the already dwindling congregation to come with them? It didn't make sense, and was received as extremely divisive.

But we thought it made perfect sense. It was exciting to think that there was so much more we could do and be a part of, without having to ask permission from the Pentecostal Assemblies of Canada.

For a while, Steve and I thought we could be a bridge between both groups. We attended the church meetings, heard everyone's concerns—which turned accusatory and heated almost immediately. We made a commitment to lead worship as much as possible, while teaching other people to become worship leaders who could take our place as soon as possible. We sat through Sunday after miserable Sunday, as each deacon took turns preaching after both pastors were gone. I'll never forget the first time I heard a woman preach from that pulpit—it had been a big deal that Grandma Dekker was a deacon to begin with, and after knowing her for years, I was looking forward to her sermon.

She immediately opened with, "Don't worry, I asked my husband's permission first," and got a few chuckles.

She then spent the next hour using scripture to decry homosexuality as an abomination that would bring about the End Times.

Commitment be damned; we never went back after that.

Thankfully, Sharon, Calvin, Michelle, and a few other families we loved spending time with were among the group of people that left. It should have been amicable, but in a small town like Smithers, bitterness could grow quickly. We heard stories of Church People crossing to the other side of the street when they saw Community People, and the really beautiful events that we put on in town were avoided by the former congregation.

Wrestling with church conflict was not new to me; I'd been witnessing adults arguing over scriptures and translations since I was a child—had been a part of leadership squabbles myself as a teenager. I didn't know what the answers were, but I knew I was tired of hurting and alienating others in the name of someone who was supposed to be Love. I was tired of Hell-level stakes that required me to be right, and being honest about that was a wilderness of a different kind.

Pregnancy (2016)

In January of 2016, with a mix of fear and joy, I told Steven that I was pregnant again. We decided to keep this news a bit more of a secret this time, and we took a deep breath when we passed the eight-week mark.

At thirteen weeks, I was in the emergency room with bleeding and another "threatened miscarriage," and I couldn't believe I'd put myself through this again.

But someone had a different plan and decided to stick around. My belly started to become more and more obvious, and our community was overjoyed with us.

When I was around twenty weeks pregnant, we had an ultrasound. This is typical. The mid-pregnancy ultrasound is the anatomical scan, when the doctors check to see how the fetus is growing and you can choose to know the sex. We chose to find out, and experienced approximately one whole day of unfettered joy knowing we were going to welcome a son named Harrison Steven.

Then came the phone call. The meeting. The words, "It looks like he has Down syndrome." Followed immediately by, "It's not too late to terminate." A one-two punch to the heart.

We drove straight to Calvin and Michelle's house to cry and pray; they reassured us that no matter what, this kid was part of our family now and they'd be there every step of the way.

~

I already knew that every once in a while, something happens that makes you have to fully cancel your life. Your cares, your responsibilities, the expectations placed upon you are bulldozed by reality, and you must deal with this event for your own sanity even if you can't explain why.

For us, that time began in July of 2016.

We knew that we had no interest in terminating this pregnancy. We also knew that medical resources up north were more limited and my body was already showing signs of distress. I was measuring bigger than I was supposed to, potentially three weeks ahead. My ankles were twice their size, though I hoped that was just the summer heat.

Another ultrasound, another doctor's appointment, the actual truth.

Our sweet baby boy was possibly not okay.

My body was producing extra amounts of amniotic fluid (influencing my size)—my son's "long" bones of femur and humerus (legs and arms) were measuring significantly shorter than the rest of his body—and there appeared to be a thickening of skin around his neck. All potential markers for Down syndrome or a genetic bone disease.

While we processed this, our doctor asked if we'd be okay with getting a referral to see a specialist at BC Women's Hospital in Vancouver. We agreed, thinking that would take at least a couple of weeks to organize.

It took less than two days.

We got the call mid-week that Vancouver wanted to start seeing us the following Monday until who knew when.

So, in three days, I quit my job at the airport café, went on medical leave, cancelled all of our summer music gigs, asked my mom (who could now travel a bit more freely) to come take care of our house and animals, packed a bag, and hit the road for fourteen hours in a truck with no air conditioning.

Somehow, we landed at Steve's parent's house in one piece.

When you are in crisis mode, you learn to appreciate the unexpected gifts along the way. For us, these were a saving grace: text messages from close friends, support in "covering" our suddenly cancelled life, being offered anything we might need.

And the actual existence of BC Women's Hospital, roughly an hour away from where we were staying.

When I first entered this building, I was expecting to be intimidated by a giant slab of city concrete, filled with people we didn't know, to whom we were just another number. But instead, we were greeted by warm colours, friendly faces, and pictures of happy, healthy people with their new babies along every wall. A bit of comforting familiarity was seeing a Tim Hortons in the lobby.

First, we met with a geneticist who spent almost an hour gathering an entire family and medical history from both of us. Looking for any clues, obviously, but in the gentlest way.

After this, I was given three ultrasounds by two different doctors. We walked out for a long lunch break with another unexpected gift: a 3-D ultrasound picture. The beautiful face of our thirty-week-old son, peacefully unaware of anything except for our voices and snack time.

The doctors we met with after lunch were very kind and informative. They had spent their whole lunch hour discussing our medical histories and our ultrasound findings, and they had one major concern: the fluid in my belly. Not why it was there, but the amount: four extra litres. *Four.* I was supposed to be carrying one, but I had *five*. That's two large bottles of pop that have never been opened. As a result, this extra fluid was responsible for putting undue stress on my cervix, making it much more likely to open and cause labour *any day* rather than seven to ten weeks from now. That fluid, if I had any hope of reaching full term safely, needed to be taken out as soon as possible, through a procedure called amniocentesis and decompression. That's where they stick a pretty large needle and tube in your belly and drain as much liquid from it as they can. The liquid can be tested genetically for any health problems; the procedure can also trigger contractions, labour or miscarriage.

We had a big decision to make, and thankfully they gave us more than an hour to make it.

On any other day, if this was being offered to us just to find out if our baby was going to be born with a genetic disability, we wouldn't risk it. Disabilities changed nothing in our hearts. But the fact that he was in danger of being born so prematurely, even at the best hospital in BC, helped us make the decision: we would risk it.

So, we made the appointment and they sent us home for the day, but not before giving me a shot of steroids to help my son's lungs reach maturity faster if he was suddenly, unexpectedly brought into the world.

I was an old pro with shots by this point, so I rolled up my sleeve and held out my arm.

"Oh no, sweetie, you need to stand up. This one goes in your bum."

Oh.

She stuck me, then said, "Come back a little early for a second dose tomorrow, okay?"

Motherfucker.

"Will do. Can it go in the other cheek tomorrow? If I suddenly, finally, develop a toned ass, it'd be great to have, like, an *even* one."

We went home, had dinner, sort of slept. From 4:00 a.m. to mid-morning, I threw up a few times—nothing I wasn't used to, but now accompanied by the knowledge that there was a 50 percent chance I could go into labour today.

When we arrived at the hospital around 11:30 a.m., I discovered that not only was my friend and former roommate Jenna coming to find us for lunch, but that (because of her local nursing work connections and just general charm, probably) she would be able to spend much of the afternoon with us, during amniocentesis and all.

So, during one of the craziest hours of my life, I had a friend rubbing my shoulders, and my husband rubbing my feet while looking into my eyes. I was able to take deep breaths while doctors covered my belly with pink antiseptic, doctors-in-training watched and whispered, taking notes like we were all in an episode of *Grey's Anatomy.* I made jokes about Jenna being my partner and fellow baby mama while Steve was our most generous sperm donor, as they punctured my swollen belly. Like a fresh peach, I could feel my body's juices dripping down my sides and I prayed, *let this help, not harm. Help, not harm.*

Baby Button cooperated and stayed out of the way of the tube, but my uterus got a little irritated, causing a contraction that trapped and shook the syringe around my puncture and took my breath away for about thirty seconds.

They were able to take almost three litres of fluid before my body and Baby had enough. For the next couple of hours in recovery, I had mild contractions every ten minutes or so.

As I experienced all these new feelings and sensations, I realized that, as a doula, I'd been able to hippie-dippie the shit out of contractions and their purpose.

In my doula work I had been taught, "Every pain brings your baby that much closer, breathe in, breathe out, picture the ocean tide, picture your baby coming closer to you with each wave, that's it. You've got this."

But those affirmations didn't apply to me, not today. *I don't "got this," I don't want this. Stay back, ocean waves, keep my baby swimming a little while longer, please. Seven weeks, that's all I ask.*

My body listened. They let me go home that night, with a list of things to keep an eye on and orders to do nothing like it was my job. Our long-term plan was to stay in the Lower Mainland until Baby was born, going to ultrasounds and clinics once a week, talking about the best care he could receive once he was born, if he needed a little extra help.

I would miss having my summer in Smithers and using the brand new maternity rooms there. But I knew this was for the best. The timing of discovering that I urgently needed the amnio done, along with having ready-made family to stay with, and Steve having consistent flooring work lined up locally until September... we knew we were where we were meant to be.

And we were ready to love our little guy to pieces, whenever and however he came to us.

Until then, my sleeping and breathing had become much more blissful. Losing eight pounds of fluid overnight will do that to you.

Parenthood (2016)

Over the next eight weeks, we adapted to our new life. Steven took work when we didn't have hospital appointments, and I split my time evenly between my bed, the swimming pool, and the fro-yo place. I would receive two more amniocentesis procedures before September came; the fluid kept returning while my son grew, and the only answer we had for sure was that he didn't have Down syndrome.

After my mom joined us down south in late August, our friends back home in Smithers literally held down our fort—helping us pay rent for a place we weren't staying in, gathering firewood in our shed for the coming winter, preparing the nursery for our return. Active hope that this was just a bump in the road on the way to our happy ending.

By mid-September, I was done.

I know every third-trimester parent says that, but I was not just "uncomfortable and round and can't see my toes" level of done. I was "answering questionnaires for concerned psychiatrists/sense of humour completely gone/collapsing into tears for no reason at least once a day" done.

I had survived a fake Apocalypse. I had lived in fear of the government and deportation. I had moved houses at least as many times as I'd had birthdays. I'd seen a childhood friend die right in front of me. I had endured losing a relationship with my father two months after it began. I had gotten on airplanes by myself, lost a pregnancy, lost jobs, and been one paycheque ahead of a financial disaster for years.

But nine months of pregnancy, one of life's greatest mysteries that I was looking forward to the most, was the straw that broke this camel's back.

I felt sad. I felt angry. I felt needy. I felt weak.

And so I felt lost. My identity was shifting. I had always been the girl who writes about all the crazy shit that happens to her, and still managed to make people smile. I was Chandler Bing of the friend group, the Spartan who keeps on trucking, I was the one who has heard time and again, "Wow.

Looking at you, listening to you, I would never have guessed that you survived all *that*. You're amazing, and you should probably write a book."

My shit had always been a little messy, but it was my mess, and it made me stronger.

Now? After being pregnant and sick and worried and unprepared for 267 days in a row (including being displaced from home for over two months in a cramped house with four animals and four in-laws)?

What I wanted was to go to sleep and wake up in my own bed with a fresh mani-pedi, a killer haircut, a multi-ethnic buffet, and an impossibly adorable baby who never cries longer than five minutes or makes me question whether I am mentally and emotionally capable of becoming a mother in the first place.

I felt gross for even admitting it. Because I could picture all the ladies who have been moms for years, who were probably laughing at my innocence and thinking, "Just you wait, honey, it gets worse."

I could see all the ladies who have been thinking they'd like to get pregnant, and I had ruined it for them.

I could imagine all the ladies who had magical unicorn pregnancies with babies made from Jesus's eyelashes and were secretly judging me for being so dramatic and non-sacrificial.

On September 15, I heard those magical words, "It's time for you to be induced," followed by, "because your uterus is coming apart."

I'm not a doctor, and I don't quite remember what they said, but apparently my womb had had *quite enough* with the three decompression drains and the carrying of the child, so its linings were separating. Also, the umbilical cord's attachment to my placenta was off, and things could get gnarly for my son as soon as my water broke. Like a bath toy being too close when the plug is pulled.

I was already two centimetres dilated, so they didn't want to wait for me to go into labour naturally anymore. It was go time.

They sent us home to pack and prepare and wait for the phone call, which came at one in the afternoon the following day.

"We have an induction spot open for you. Can you be here at two o'clock?"

We were so ready.

I don't know how we made it to Vancouver from Langley in less than an hour, but we did. My mind was whirling.

I'm having a baby today. Maybe. And we're not travelling by ambulance; this is like a planned event. Oh God, is this like that thing where you're supposed to be careful what you wish for? What's Steve thinking about? What if I can't do this?

Sirius kept sending me texts and pictures to reassure me that I could indeed do this.

By three o'clock, I was gowned like a queen, sitting atop my button-controlled throne, ready to receive my Cervidil tampon.

This was step one. If you're not sure what I'm talking about, remember where tampons go. And then imagine that it's covered with this sticky gel called prostaglandin that makes dilation continue slowly, sometimes over a period of twenty-four hours—to be followed by a fresh tampon if necessary. If things are really taking their sweet time, an IV of oxytocin to simulate contractions would be step two. (Typically, once one receives the tampon, they go home to wait it out and come back. But since we weren't local, we were admitted to stay until the sweet, sweet end.)

We prepared to sit there for a long time. I tried to think big, billowy, open-y thoughts while eating a chicken Caesar salad. For four hours, I experienced normal mild cramping, which made me excited and also a bit self-satisfied that I could totally handle this.

And then? Nothing. Not a peep or a twinge for hours. We got bored. We marvelled at what people did before hospitals got free wi-fi. We prepared to try and sleep.

Just before eleven o'clock, something happened that I can only describe as being headbutted in the bladder, followed by an immense relief of pressure and the unpleasantness of water gushing out of me to cover the entire bed.

I'm not exaggerating. The *entire* bed.

I whispered to Steve very calmly that I believed my water had broken, before I doubled over in agony.

We pressed the magic button and the nurse came in and took in the scene. Her eyes widened and she said, "Okay, so I'll be your nurse from now on, and we're going to gently move you to another room. You are having a baby before my shift is over, my dear."

I did the math... it was 11:00 p.m.... shifts change over at 7:00 a.m.... *what?*

"But this is my first baby! I'm supposed to have another Cervidil tomorrow, maybe an oxytocin IV!" My voice getting higher with each word.

"Your baby is ready to come without any of that, sweetie. It's a good thing you were already here."

For the next hour, everything else that needed to be done was patterned by contractions: do something productive, like remove the Cervidil tampon—have a backstabbing contraction; start a conversation—have a backstabbing contraction; move out the door and into the hallway—have a backstabbing contraction.

Surely, it would be over soon.

At one in the morning, in my new room, a doctor checked my cervix.

"Four centimetres dilated! Coming along nicely."

I nearly started crying. All that time, all that pain, and I still had six centimetres to go. Oh, and then I still had to PUSH the baby out!

I had a quick little talk with myself: *Every day, for the past thirty-eight weeks and four days, you have vomited. You have been in the emergency room twice, for bleeding and dehydration. You've been drained of amniotic fluid three times, injected with steroids four times, and stayed three nights in hospital. You've been poked and prodded and worried and afraid and bored out of your mind on bedrest, away from the home and community you love—surrounded by healthcare professionals you have never met. And now, for better or for worse, it's almost over.*

Girl. Treat yourself.

I smiled, made my decision and opened my mouth: "I'd like an epidural as soon as possible, please."

The next few hours were pretty blissful. Sure, I couldn't use my legs and I was peeing into a bag, but the pain was gone. We were by ourselves, the lights were dim, the machines were quiet. We passed the time talking in half-asleep tones. My ability to cope was slowly returning.

At four in the morning, everything changed. Much to everyone's surprise, I had gone from four centimetres dilated to ten in three hours, despite an epidural's tendency to slow things down.

All of a sudden, the lights got a little brighter. Machinery and doctors started materializing until the room was packed.

Ready or not, it was time for me to start pushing.

I recall what happened in the next forty-two minutes with a dream-like quality, almost as if it happened to someone else.

I have no way of accurately explaining what it's like to push a baby out of your body when you can't see anything and you can't feel anything.

I do know that I had my useless legs propped up by a nurse and my anything-but-useless husband, and that they helped squeeze-fold me in half every time I contracted.

Steve was my superhero. I had been a little worried about him, but he stepped up majorly, even looking *down there* to see the baby's head and tell me there was dark hair, when he'd said multiple times beforehand that he'd keep his eyes on my face the whole time for both our sakes.

The tone of the room changed. Instead of hearing "You're doing an amazing job, Carly!" like I had been, I heard, "Vitals are dipping... something's not right... possible c-section... can we get forceps in here?"

A few moments later, a new doctor appeared, checked me, said, "Yep, let's go get him—forceps!"

"Okay, Carly, we're gonna make a little slice here to help assist the forceps... and then you push as hard as you can on your next contraction."

Too hopped up on adrenaline to worry or realize I'd just received an episiotomy, I did just that. My belly tightened, I strained, and then... "Stop pushing! The cord's wrapped around his neck."

I saw scissors, I heard a snip and them telling me to push one more time... but I didn't hear any crying.

My heart stopped as they placed a gooey, slightly blue little boy on my chest.

Less than fifteen seconds later, they took him away to a table surrounded by NICU staff to stabilize him.

The only thought in my head was, *He's perfect. From his dark curly head down to his ten little toes, he's absolutely perfect. And they were so worried.*

Steve stood near the NICU table, trying to take in what was happening. I was receiving stitches and waiting for my placenta to come out.

When it did, it was in pieces. I'm not sure why. Apparently, my body had been just as done being pregnant as I was. As soon as my water broke, the self-destruct button was pushed.

Over and over again, we thanked God we had already been at the hospital. Over and over, I thanked myself for getting that epidural. Nothing else could have helped me get through the war zone my flesh and blood was going to become.

We didn't know how long it would be before we were allowed to see Harrison, so we were escorted to our room just as the sun came up. Somehow, Steve fell asleep on a cot next to my bed; I sat up in the bed, still bloody and sweaty and sticky. The nurse had left a little bag of toiletries, as well as a tube to collect my first milk in. She had shown me how to cup my breast with my hand, but I forgot the rest of her instructions. Tears seeped out of my eyes as I squeezed my nipples over and over, to no milky avail. Somewhere in this hospital, my son was wrapped up and sleeping alone. He needed food; I needed to make it for him. So why couldn't I?

Six hours later, we were finally called to come see our son again, this time in the Newborn Intensive Care Unit (NICU) nursery.

Twelve hours later, he was off the oxygen, and we were able to hold him for the first time. I was weepy and felt like I wasn't there at the same time. Like I was watching myself from up above become a mom, and it didn't feel quite right.

We didn't know it then, but we had just completed day one of twenty-three.

NICU and Diagnosis (2016)

For the first twenty-three days of his life, Harrison was kept in an environment that never relaxed even for one second. Lights and machines were always on, babies were always making noise, it was always hot, and there was barely enough room between NICU cribs to fit just one chair that was comfortable enough to try nursing in. Sleeping there was out of the question, but leaving him in the hospital every night for twenty-three nights felt impossible. Our local Ronald McDonald House on site was full, so our social worker arranged for us to stay at Easter Seals House, a few blocks away. It was next to Safeway, and our room came with a little kitchenette and TV. We would spend twelve hours in the NICU with our newborn, and then inexplicably leave to go shopping, to cook, to distract ourselves with reality TV for a couple of hours before falling into another broken sleep. We had Steve's family deliver a breast pump to us so that my milk had somewhere to go; instead of having a baby to wake me up, I relied on an alarm to rouse me every two hours so I could pump and store the milk in our fridge. Every morning, I would pack it up in a cooler like it was liquid gold and quickly transport it to the NICU freezer. And then every two hours, I would try to nurse him and he would hate it and I would cry, and then I'd leave his side to try to find a quiet enough place to keep pumping. Meanwhile, I was still healing from my episiotomy, so I also carried a "donut" cushion with me wherever I went to help me sit comfortably.

Twenty-three days of blood tests, x-rays, ultrasounds, an MRI, machines and sick babies.

Twenty-three days of taking in the other families around us, worn with the battles of fighting for lives that were too fragile to fight for themselves.

Twenty-three days of doctors and nurses who truly cared, almost to the point of making us crazy at how long everything seemed to be taking.

But in the end, it was another blessing in disguise. Because after twenty-three days, our little Harrison Steven was given hope to live as well as he could with a diagnosis called Noonan syndrome. A genetic disorder similar to Down Syndrome, but instead of adding an extra chromosome to your DNA, it deletes a pair. And depending on which pair is deleted, Noonan syndrome affects every body differently. We made the mistake of googling it, finding stark images of children with twisted spines and enlarged heads and scars from heart transplants, if they survived.

The final blood test Harrison had, the lab compared it with a sample of my blood and Steve's blood; this technology had not existed even six months beforehand. We discovered that neither Steve nor I had been a carrier of this syndrome; the mutation was random. Parenting never came with a manual even on the easiest of days, and we were jumping into medical parenting without a parachute. We would soon learn from our geneticists that they didn't know everything about Noonan syndrome yet either, but they did know that it had been sorted into four main "types," and Harrison belonged to the type RAF1—the rarest but allegedly mildest type.

It seemed to be manifesting itself mostly in a few unique physical features (which we found adorable) and one extra-thick heart muscle. Of course, that could change over time. But ultimately, it was the answer to all our questions, and we would take each challenge as it came. His cardiologist and any other doctors we needed were going to walk us through every step of his slower-than-typical growth and development, and we could expect a lot of resources from Vancouver and our local Smithers Early Childhood Educators.

Since he was diagnosed so early, we could now make a treatment plan and take him back home to Smithers to introduce him to all his loved ones as early as November.

We felt so ready.

Postpartum (2017)

As a cisgender woman growing up in the evangelical church, I had been involved in childcare and dreaming about becoming a mother nearly my whole life, so now that I was in my late twenties and Harrison was finally here, I was ready for the feelings of fulfilment to arrive. Instead, I was met with failure after failure.

I had hated the NICU while Harrison was there, but I learned to resent it once we were home. After twenty-three days there, it felt like Harrison had loved it. Bringing him home to a room that was often quiet and dimly lit, and having full breasts at his comfortable beck and call made him very angry. And I wept more, imagining him asking us to take him back there instead of being at home with us.

For us, Harrison crying was never just a baby crying that we could comfort and he would be okay even if he cried for a while. Crying for Harrison meant blood vessels bulging in his face and an unsafe increased heart rate. Keeping him calm and happy for as long as possible was our mandate, and I—the one who was built to feed and comfort and care for this new human—could never quite accomplish that.

Meanwhile, Steve—who had never held a baby before in his life—was Harrison's best friend. I had my moments, though. I took him for walks, and put him on the couch next to me while I mixed a batch of cookie dough. When he was finally strong enough to hold up his own head independently at six months, I strapped him to my chest in a sling and felt a bit of freedom returning. It was difficult to ever feel safe taking eyes off of him, but it was also deeper than that; watching Harrison discover the world made my life better, and I wanted him to be a part of everything.

During our unexpected time in the Lower Mainland, Steve had become reacquainted with his lifelong work of laying floors, and his contractors were eager to have him back. Smithers was a little more complicated to break into the trades; lumber yards and contractors already had their teams very well established. So, to keep us going, Steve did what many parents in the remote North were required to do: leave home for work every two weeks and then return for two weeks, over and over. It was the last thing in the world he wanted to do, but I reassured him that Harrison and I would be all right.

Steve was gone for four days when I had to rush Harrison to the local hospital.

He had been sniffling and coughing all through the night, and while I figured he just had his first cold, I was still living half an hour from town and needed reassurance.

We waited in the emergency room for a few hours and Harrison finally slept. Steve and I were constantly texting back and forth, and some friends brought me food. Doctors who had never heard of noonan Syndrome were on the phone with our Children's Hospital doctors and taking tests; I was one breath away from telling Steve to come home.

The tests came back with a diagnosis of RSV, a very common infection that babies often get and typically always survive. Anyone else might have been sent home with a prescription of extra-strength Tylenol, but we were admitted for five days. Steve stayed down south because he knew we could be flown down to Children's at any moment.

I had an in-person community who wore masks so that they could regularly bring me food and clothes, an online community of Noonan syndrome parents that I could draw strength from, and the most supportive husband I could ask for—and still, I faltered.

After four days without sleep, watching my little boy struggle to breathe or eat, wiping his nose, administering a nebulizer, rocking him until my arms went numb while he screamed—who I was completely left me.

Afraid of dropping him, I put him down on the bed. I started pacing and muttering, "Go to sleep, just please go to sleep," over and over, getting a little louder with each round of the room. My words escalated and turned into sobs while Harrison wailed on the bed. Six months' worth of failures started to rage through me, and I slapped myself across the face, back and forth, back and forth until my ears rang. It felt good to release, to feel, to finally show on the outside what I was feeling on the inside.

I guess we were a little too loud because a nurse came in and gently removed me from the room.

This is it, I thought. *Someone has finally realized I'm not meant to be a mother, and they're taking me to the psychiatric ward so I don't hurt my baby.*

The thought of this was actually a relief—maybe silence and sleep were in my future. Maybe Harrison would have a better mom, finally.

But the nurse led me to a little sanctuary room with a couch and a blanket. "I'll watch Harrison for a while. You try to get some rest."

I tried to smile through my puffy face and act like everything about this was absolutely normal.

Sleep did not come. My cheeks were sore with my anger, and my brain would not stop racing. For the first time that I could recall, I was scared of me.

The following day, we were able to go home and I felt the pieces of my role and purpose slowly returning. Steve came home the following week, promising to never leave us again.

Awakening (2017)

By the summer of 2017, I was starting to feel a little more grounded in my motherhood. After being in danger and then recovering for over a year, my body was starting to feel like herself again too, to my relief. I would never be the same, but it felt right.

So, I invited my long-time friend Sirius to come up from Colorado and stay with us over the July long weekend. I knew that another friend, Maria, was going to be driving up around the same time, so we arranged for Sirius to catch a ride.

Maria was a few years older than me and had been about to graduate out of the youth group at the church by the time I joined. She was bright and bubbly and deep as a river; we had always enjoyed staying in touch over the years.

Introducing Maria and Sirius to each other, having them get along so well, and having them witness my beautiful son was like a balm on my raw heart. We made food, we hiked and played outside, we watched comedy specials, and on their last night, Steven took Harrison so we could have a little party.

Sirius and Maria had been staying out in our old camper in the yard every night for the past week, but that last night, I joined them—with a bottle of wine. I hadn't been off-duty from being a mom, a medical mom, for the past ten months, and I planned to enjoy myself a little.

They did too. I laughed in shock as Maria revealed that she'd brought supplies to get high but had no idea what to do with them. We laughed in ridiculous delight as Sirius said, "I guess we're googling how to roll a joint."

I'd never inhaled smoke into my body in any way at all before, except maybe by accident over the campfire and wood stove. I didn't know how, and it took all my concentration. I passed the joint to Maria, my eyes following it to her lips ever so quickly before glancing away. I wanted to focus on my wine instead.

The more Sirius and Maria drank and smoked, the sillier they got. They got on the bed and started posing, alternating between sultry and ridiculous. "Take pictures of us for our dating profiles," they giggled at me, tossing me their phones. Their giggling was contagious, and I went into director mode, telling them how to sit on the bed and trying to get a good angle in absolutely dreadful camper lighting.

Before long, Maria flung off her shirt and said, "This will be a good one!" as she squished her breasts between her hands to make even more cleavage for her glamour shot.

"God, it's like watching Kate Winslet in *Titanic*, but in real life," Sirius quipped.

God, it really was. I gulped. Was the camper getting warmer? Probably just the wine hitting my brain. I tried to cancel the buzzing noise in my head by holding up Maria's camera phone and saying, "I'll draw you like one of my French girls."

Maria and Sirius burst out cackling. "Okay, me too," Sirius said before taking off their shirt. Seeing them half naked didn't hit me the same for some reason. Maybe it was just a one-off feeling of surprise.

I took a few more pictures, and then Maria convinced me to be in them as well. One caveat: my shirt should go. Continuity and all that. "Free that nipple, mama!" she laughed, her eyes sparkling.

I wasn't the same awkward young woman who had played strip poker and could barely look her friends in the eye. I was even further from the little girl who had played Ken to her friends' Barbie just so she didn't get left out. I was married, I'd quite nakedly had a baby in front of fourteen medical professionals less than a year ago. Bodies were just bodies, and they were nice, and I wanted to have fun.

"Free the nipple," I replied, taking off my shirt. Maria and Sirius cheered.

We spent another hour in the camper just drinking and talking and taking silly pictures; the one joint we'd managed to roll was long burnt out. It was so liberating to just enjoy this night with my friends, be myself, know that my family was safe, and God wasn't angry.

Almost drawn like a magnet, we all sleepily laid down in a cuddle puddle on the bed. I was closest to the wall, with Sirius in the middle; since Maria was closest to the edge of the bed, she reached up to turn the light off. As she snuggled back down next to us, we all draped our arms across each other, heads leaning, ready for sleep. My hand had landed half-drunkenly on Maria's right upper arm and right breast. I didn't move it, and she didn't shift.

She was so, so soft. Without thinking, I started stroking her arm with my thumb like I was comforting her to sleep. She let out a quiet pleasant hum, and still didn't move. Eventually, my thumb stroke went wider and wider, going from one side of her arm all the way across her perfect breast, even reaching her nipple a few times. It felt a little more raised every time my thumb came back; was I causing that? My entire body felt like it was on fire, and I didn't know why, and I didn't want to stop. Against everything I'd been taught and contorted myself into for decades, I wanted to touch my friend, a woman. And I knew it.

You have a husband and a baby in the house, you absolute whore.

I sat up in the bed, trying to get through the tangle of arms and legs, my body feeling like it was on fire but for a different reason now. Somehow in the dark, I found my shirt. There were two beds, but Maria and Sirius stayed where they were. That was fine. Maybe none of us would remember this in the morning.

I entered the house, breathing a sigh of relief when I didn't hear any activity. My beautiful family was asleep, and I barely deserved to be in the same house as them.

I crawled into bed, immediately surrounded by the familiar comfort of Steven's warmth. I wrapped myself like a big spoon around him; I still wanted to touch his body so much too. What in the world was wrong with me? Leftover breastfeeding hormones? The wine? Maybe I'd managed to get high after all.

My last thought before drifting off to sleep was that even if Maria and Sirius didn't remember this night, I knew I would remember it for the rest of my life.

Abbotsford (2017–2018)

By Harrison's first birthday that September, we couldn't deny it anymore: we couldn't stay in Smithers. We had to move back to the Lower Mainland. Steve's work was really coming through for us and being close to all of Harrison's specialists would help bring us some peace of mind.

Around the same time, a friend of ours going through a very sudden divorce posted on Facebook that he was looking for roommates so that he and his dog could keep his house in Abbotsford. Without really thinking it through, we replied immediately. Abbotsford was thirty minutes away from Steve's family and most of his work; finding a place to rent (that was also okay with a baby *and* Poppy and Walter) was one of the most challenging parts about moving to the Lower Mainland.

For the last fifteen months, absolutely nothing had gone according to plan. Dreams, goals, aspirations, thoughts, hopes... all twisted and turned into a maze that had led us here. Starting over. My childhood story of never getting attached to a person, place or thing—that I thought would heal with time and evidence of safety—began another chapter.

~

The move felt really real when the new tenant moved into our northern paradise one fall weekend. After Steve and his dad made a couple of trips back and forth to transport our belongings, we were officially out.

There were so many things I wanted to say. I wish I'd walked through the woods and the streets more. I wish I'd looked at that mountain more, touched the river more. I wish I'd said "thank you for your help" better, and "let's go for coffee" and actually done it.

We moved into Joe's basement in late September of 2017. It consisted of one bedroom, one bathroom, one living room and a room where there could have been—should have been—a kitchenette with a stack washer and dryer. We put Harrison's crib in the bedroom because it had a door we could close, and we squeezed our queen bed plus a mini fridge into the "dining room" area.

Joe and two other men who had also experienced sudden relationship changes shared the top two floors. We called it Heartbreak Hotel, and we tried to mind our own business underneath their chaos.

Whenever laundry needed to be done, I would carry full baskets up and down two flights of stairs, hoping no other roommates were using it at the time I needed it. The kitchen was also shared between all of us, and every night, I would carry dishes up and down the stairs to my new best friend: the dishwasher.

While all the men were at work during the day, Harrison and I would hang out on the main floor, just to get some space. Harrison learned to climb on those stairs; the following year, he would take his first steps in that kitchen too.

We spent our time taking Poppy to the nearby dog park, a place where she could run free like she used to—and once I got my hard-earned bearings for driving around the city, I bundled Harrison up to go to the Duft & Co bakery or the Superstore; the library or a playgroup that featured sign language. I watched his hair and teeth and confidence blossom right before my eyes, his dimpled smile and soft golden-brown curls warming my heart. I was lonely and sad and bone-tired, but Abbotsford started to feel like it could become home.

One chilly November morning, I let Poppy out into our backyard and went about my day. As often happens this close to the coast, a rainstorm appeared out of nowhere, and I thought nothing of it. Hours passed, and by mid-afternoon, I got an unexpected phone call from Steve.

"Have you seen Poppy?" he asked. "The neighbours next door just called me, saying they have her and got my number from her collar."

My stomach dropped out. "Oh my goodness, I let her out this morning, and completely forgot to let her back in. The rainstorm..."

I hung up, wrapped Harrison on my back, and went outside, noting the broken gate. Forgetting the dog wasn't like me at all. Panicking and running away during a storm, however, was absolutely like Poppy. Poor thing.

I knocked on the neighbour's door, and a kindly woman in her forties named Jackie answered the door. "Oh! I have Poppy! She's playing in the backyard!"

I began a long, apologetic speech, thanking her for taking our drenched pup in. I needn't have felt too badly; Poppy was having the time of her life racing around a massive backyard garden with a little bulldog named Pablo Escobar.

"This is a gorgeous garden. Did you build this?" I asked as we watched the dogs playing.

"Yes, my husband and I moved here from Jamaica last year, and Pablo is our only child, so we spend most of our time working out here." Jackie played peek-a-boo with Harrison, immediately winning him over.

I wanted to stay and inquire more, but the November sun was already setting, and I would need to get Poppy cleaned up and settled back home so I could start dinner.

"Again, thank you so much, Jackie. It isn't the first time this has happened, but it appears Poppy has more lives than a cat."

She grinned from ear to ear. "Absolutely no problem. Bring Poppy and Harrison over again sometime when it's a little warmer!"

A couple of absent-minded weeks later, on a hunch, I took a pregnancy test and it was positive. *Well, that explains that.*

Evie-Rey (2018)

Even though I had been pregnant less than two years ago, and everything about the experience had been incredibly stressful, we were thrilled to be welcoming a sibling for Harrison. This had been planned, but not expected to "take" so quickly.

Because of my health history, I was seen exclusively by the doctors at BC Women's Hospital for the first twenty weeks, just to be sure. It was kind of nice; Steve would take the day off, we'd drop Harrison off at his grandparents, and then we'd drive into the city. After my appointment, we'd go for a drive, have some food, and see the ocean. It became like a Date Day tradition.

At our final appointment with BC Women's, I had an ultrasound. I heard three things: everything looked very healthy this time, it appeared as though a girl was developing, and "We spotted a small fibroid on the outside of your uterus. Nothing to worry about but keep an eye on it." They then gave me a referral for a maternity doctor in Abbotsford and sent me on my way.

It quickly became apparent that we would need more space, and since two of the three men in Heartbreak Hotel had moved on, we made an agreement with Joe to switch floors. On Easter weekend, Elijah and Jenna came over and helped us move our sparse basement belongings upstairs. Even though I couldn't do much except feed the helpers, it felt like the best day of my life. We could prepare ourselves this time, Harrison had his own room again, I had a kitchen again, and for the first time in our six-year marriage, we had more than one bathroom. Heaven.

Not long after that, my mom made plans to come down from Hyder to stay with us and help in any way she could. I knew what day she was coming and that it would likely be at night, but I got a little more worried with each hour that passed. Steve went to bed. I stayed up reading, listening for a car to pull into the driveway.

Finally, just before midnight, I heard it. I excitedly got to the front door as fast as I could, opened it, and stopped in my tracks.

An almost unrecognizable woman was hobbling up my front steps, using a long stick in each hand and groaning in pain.

Sure, it had been a while since I'd seen her, but Dorothy Jean Butler had been a Spartan every single day of my life and now—after seven years in Hyder, Alaska—she looked like a prisoner of war. Fear fought for a place in my belly next to my unborn daughter.

I got her settled into bed, and she seemed so relieved, lightly caressing my belly. "Mom, are you all right?"

She laughed it off. "Oh yeah, my joints just aren't what they used to be, and I use up way more energy now so I lost about fifty pounds. I needed to, anyway!"

Your cheeks are sunken in, I thought. I wanted to feed her and get her into a warm bath, but even if we'd had a tub on the main floor, I'm not sure she would have been able to get back out.

"We'll get you to a doctor soon," I said, tucking her in.

"Oh, you've got enough to worry about, babe. Besides, I already saw a doctor in Stewart and I had to leave because she kept asking me the most inappropriate questions. I'm fine, I promise."

I didn't want to leave it, but I would soon have no choice but to. I knew one thing, however: there was no way my mom was going back to Hyder, Alaska.

~

My current pregnancy was so average that I forgot I was even pregnant multiple times. Right up until week thirty-eight, when I dealt with prodromal labour multiple times—even resorting to a membrane sweep to try and make things happen.

Our due date was June 25, 2018. Of course, she gave me peace and quiet the whole day, after two weeks of pure hell. But I woke up the next day, and I knew something would be different. By dinnertime that evening, I was ordering a pizza to come to the house to feed Mom and us on our way out the door to the hospital. "If it's not real labour this time, I'm demanding a c-section," I said through gritted teeth.

I did not need to demand anything. I could barely walk to our hospital room without doubling over in agony every two minutes, and I asked Heidi the nurse to prepare an epidural post-haste.

"I don't do that," she answered honestly. "But I will find someone who does."

The next few hours were bliss, and since it was a fairly quiet night, we had a chance to chat with Heidi while we reminisced about the last time I had given birth. She got an earful, about how there had been fourteen other doctors and nurses, forceps, a wrapped umbilical cord, and a NICU stay. "I honestly don't care who's here or what happens tonight, as long as everything is good," I said. Birth plans are for the privileged few.

The doctor came in around eleven o'clock that evening and checked me. "Well, that's fun," he said. "Your baby's going to be born on my daughter's birthday."

"Oh, is that tomorrow?" I chuckled.

"There's one hour of it left," he said, smiling.

Our eyes widened. There was no way.

But that doctor knew his shit, because at exactly 11:55 p.m., I reached down between my legs and pulled my daughter Evangeline Rey to my chest in disbelief.

Her dark eyes, exactly like mine, stared up at me, and I laugh-sobbed as I realized that no one was coming to whisk her away. She was breathing, and she was staying with me. The euphoria was enough to make me float away.

I saw Heidi the nurse wipe her eyes as she said, "Every birth is special, but this one feels a little more so after hearing your story."

In a completely unprecedented action, we brought our baby home less than twenty-four hours later.

A gift we would never take for granted.

My Body Is a Badass (2018)

Something about giving birth this time was different. With Harrison, I was grateful to be alive, and it took a lot of time to reacquaint myself with my body. I had been stitched up differently than I used to be, I felt muscles and tendons and nerves all over that I'd never accessed before.

With Evie, I was strong. I had adapted, and I felt more capable. I had literally pulled her from my own body and taken her home less than twenty-four hours later. After decades of being terrified of my hips and breasts and vulva, I was a goddess with the scars to prove it. I thought back to twelve-year-old me in the woods, bleeding for the first time, facing adulthood with no relief from it except the hope of Tylenol and fresh water.

Sirius came to visit us in Abbotsford, and I had a chance to tell them how things were going. "I feel like I finally started to break the curse of self-hatred in my brain," I said. "I think my body is beautiful, and anyone who doesn't want to see it can just pluck their own eyes out."

Sirius got a twinkle in their eye. "I love that for you, mama. And… if I can say it… I think you've liked boobs for a little longer than just recently."

My face went red. "Wait. You remember that?"

"Are you serious? Of course I do, I was sandwiched right between you and Maria—I literally saw the whole thing."

I was flustered. "I'm really sorry about that. I don't know what came over me."

"Oh honey, it's okay, I think you might be bi!"

"Bi? What, like, bisexual? I'm not even sure that's real. My mom likes to say every politician has to be bisexual and sleep their way to the top, so I thought it was just another one of her conspiracy theories."

Sirius rolled their eyes. "Of course she thinks that. I promise you that being bi is nothing more than being attracted to more than one gender. It doesn't have to be a big deal."

The more I thought about it, they were right. I'd often secretly thought to myself that I couldn't actually be queer because I was only obsessed with boobs, not... anywhere else. But ever since I stopped hating and being afraid of my own body, I stopped hating and being afraid of other bodies too.

I loved a cisgender man, but I adored the ground that cisgender women, nonbinary people, transgender people and two-spirit people walked on.

~

Being a mother of two under two was exactly as chaotic as everyone had said it would be. Perhaps even more so, as they were both what I would call sensitive, often at the same time. In many ways, I felt like a new parent all over again, as everything about raising Evie-Rey was different than raising Harrison. She grew and developed like a typical baby, and it almost went by too fast to appreciate. Harrison and Evie-Rey brought me such joy; every new day I got to share with them, I felt grateful anew that I had followed a different path out of the woods so long ago—that the world had continued long enough, safely enough, to give them life.

Evie-Rey was about three months old when we started to feel really settled into our routine. While Evie adored Harrison, Harrison alternated between being really gentle with Evie, to having a difficult time hearing her cry. And she cried a lot.

Taking him to an Ear, Nose and Throat specialist started to give us a fuller picture of not only his mild-to-moderate hearing loss in one ear, but also how certain sounds were received. We did everything we could to meet their conflicting access needs, but it was often more than we were prepared for.

We decided to take them on their first road trip together back home to Smithers just before my thirty-first birthday. It was so heart-filling to be surrounded by family, to have my babies witnessed by the people who meant the most to me. We had family photos taken and showed the kids all of "our" places—including Main Street for coffee at the kiosk Bugwood Bean. It's a lovely outdoor area on the corner, with a little hut in the style of a log cabin and little picnic tables arranged on the sidewalk. Evie was still waking up every few hours, and a cup of Bugwood-level coffee felt like the only thing that could keep me going.

We had only been gone for a year, but we were pleasantly surprised to arrive at Bugwood Bean and see a rainbow sidewalk connecting to the doctor's clinic. The first Pride Society had been formed just after we moved away—and for the first time in my life, I wondered if all of me could be seen, would be welcome here. My heart started pounding really hard every time I thought about actually saying the words, "I'm bisexual." I knew there would be questions and rejections and just plain not understanding. Yes, I was married to a cisgender man. Yes, I was a mother to two children. Yes, I was happy. Why did it matter?

It mattered because I was finally in a place where I wanted to be honest, to let people in, to shine a light and make myself visible because there was actually nothing to be ashamed of. I was filled with the desire to normalize every part of my identity, because I *was* normal. I'd spent enough time hiding; now I wanted to seek.

It was the eve of my thirty-first birthday when I decided to tell my husband. I knew there were risks. He could be hurt, or angry. He could believe I was doomed to Hell. He could leave me and take my children with him. He could be comforted by others as the poor man with a gay wife.

But I knew through my bones that he would never physically hurt me. I had to try.

We were snuggled up and sleepy after making love, and I decided that was my opportunity. His arm was wrapped around me and I laid my head on his shoulder, happy to be close enough to whisper in the dark.

"I want to tell you something."

"Hmm?" He replied sleepily. "I'm awake."

"You know I love you. You make me happy. I'm attracted to you, obviously. You know that, right?"

"Yeah. But it's always nice to know that more often." His hand rubbed up and down my arm and breast, like I had done to Maria little more than a year before. I would tell him everything.

"Well, I'm really nervous to tell you because I don't know what you'll think..."

"You can tell me anything, love."

"I think I'm what's called bisexual? I love you, I'm attracted to you, but I'm also attracted to people who aren't men, and I've been fighting it my whole life. I'm so tired of fighting."

The dark hung silent for a moment. And then… "Yeah, I can see that." Not judgment, not celebration, just observation. Was I finally being seen?

"You can?"

"Yeah, not to steal your thunder or anything, but it's been kind of obvious for a while. We're always saying the same actresses are hot. It's cool."

The breath and seemingly blood I'd been holding came back into my body with a whoosh.

"Okay. Can I tell you how I figured it out?"

I then proceeded to tell him about the night with Sirius and Maria in the camper.

"I'm really sorry," I said. "I talked to Maria too, and we're good. I don't have a thing for her, she just… put the pieces together, I guess."

Another heavy pause.

"I mean," Steven said. "She *does* have great boobs."

Unexpectedly, laughter. "She really does."

"I love you, I support you. Just remember that you're married to *me*."

"I will," I said, feeling about a thousand times lighter. Even if nobody else understood, it didn't matter, as long he knew me.

~

After telling Steve and being so well accepted, I often regret the way I chose to come out to everyone else, even though I know there's no one right way to do it. I casually slipped it into my birthday social media post, and let the chips fall where they may. And they sure did. Many people I'd known for years quietly unfollowed and unfriended me. One friend messaged me that I was cheating on Steven simply by being proud of my queerness, and another friend went so far as to send me a devotional book in the mail about "How to Interpret the Bible Correctly." I was hurt, but I understood. This is what we had been taught to do when someone we loved was in spiritual danger. I didn't know how to explain to them that I finally felt a little safer.

After some time passed, I did a "Coming Out" podcast interview with a fellow queer femme, and then sent it to my mom in an email at home while Steven and I were attending hospital appointments with Harrison downtown. I could barely eat the whole day, waiting for her response.

I listened to your interview; thank you for sharing it with me. I want to say that I love you and I'm sorry for all the ways I was emotionally unavailable to you when you were growing up. It has likely contributed to some of your beliefs now. I'm praying for both of us to heal.

It was honestly better than I expected.

I wish now that I'd been louder. Bolder. Thrown a party. It's what I deserved after hating this part of me for so long. I didn't know it yet, but I was stepping into a path that had been paved for me by my ancestors—the ones who knew that queerness was closer to Creator, not further. I was breaking generational cycles, and teaching my children a better way, just by being myself.

The re-alignment and relief this confession brought to my body and soul was immediate.

Harrison's First Surgery (2019)

Over the winter of 2018 and 2019, we made a mistake.

We took some time off. We, including all of Harrison's doctors, saw how well he was doing and for six months, we relaxed. We watched little Evie-Rey continue to grow, we had Christmas holidays, we enjoyed a rare snow day.

In February we took Harrison into the city for his cardiology check-up, and they sent us home after putting a twenty-four-hour heart Holter monitor on him.

Harrison had worn a heart Holter monitor like this twice now, so all of us knew what to expect. He was annoyed with the stickers and mesh shirt at first, but he got used to it, and we recorded all of his activities in a little journal. Then we returned the Holter and journal and waited two weeks for the results.

They were bittersweet. The good news: Harrison had gained three pounds and grown three inches since August, which was huge for him.

Unfortunately, that growth really stressed out his heart. And since we didn't know that, we had still been religiously giving him the same amount of meds three times a day, as though he hadn't grown at all. It wasn't enough.

The heart Holter showed a 15 percent increase in irregular heart-beats—even while he was asleep. He hadn't even progressed to running, jumping, climbing and horsing around like other kids! He was at the point where activity like that could seriously endanger him.

We beat ourselves up for not taking him in sooner. All we could do was slowly up the dosage of his heart meds. For this process, he would need to be hospitalized and constantly monitored. We would plan to learn CPR and ask that all of his regular caregivers do the same. And all of his future appointments would happen at BC Children's instead of going to the local hospital in Abbotsford.

We hoped this would stave off the stress on his little heart. Ultimately, the only permanent fix was a transplant, and we were ready to advocate for that action if necessary.

~

In March of 2019, we decided to bite the bullet and take Harrison to the dentist. At two and a half years of age, he had a full mouth of teeth, but his near-constant sensory struggle to having his face touched made it nearly impossible to brush his teeth like we needed to. Add to that a dose of heart medicine full of sugar three times a day, and we knew his little mouth would be in trouble soon, if not already.

The dentists at BC Children's Hospital decided the safest and easiest way to get a look at his teeth would be to sedate him and prepare for surgery. They suspected his front eight teeth were the most vulnerable and would need to go.

We were a wreck. His beautiful smile that we adored was about to completely change, and yet we knew for his safety, it needed to be done, and one day, he would understand. I hoped in my heart that by the time he started losing the rest of his teeth and growing adult ones, he'd be ready to try brushing his teeth on his own.

The next day, surgery took twice as long as planned, and for good reason: not only had they needed to remove his front eight teeth, but all his teeth except two. He kept one on each side at the very back. They'd capped them with silver in the hopes they could be saved as he got older. We had no idea when the rest of his teeth would grow.

The waiting, the knowing that long sedation took a toll on his heart and the unexpected results felt devastating to us. I found myself recalling my own medical and dental needs as a child, the lengths Mom had gone to, to ensure that I was "healthy" enough to survive an Apocalypse. Nothing could have prepared me to be relying on a mostly-free medical system to keep my child alive since before he was born.

We took Harrison home to Abbotsford with an arsenal of meds and antibiotics in syringes to gently give him until he would be ready to eat again. His face was swollen, with little bits of stitching string trailing out of his mouth.

We knew he was starting to feel like himself again when, after three days, he saw one of his favourite cartoons and it made him laugh. Our pattern of taking our emotional cues from him was solidified, and we permitted ourselves to laugh a little again too.

~

Often, in my "down time," I went online and collaborated with Noonan syndrome parents. It was such a relief but also a challenge because the variations of genetic anomalies had created such a diverse group of kids. Even if someone had the same RAF1 type as Harrison, their experience might be completely different from his.

And sometimes, I went online just to ignore my worries for a while. I was starting to build a chosen family on Twitter and Instagram, Facebook becoming the inappropriate uncle I no longer wanted to spend more than five minutes with at a party.

But I tried to follow all the same people across the board. And on Twitter, there was a page called Noonan Syndrome Hub. They didn't post often, but when they did, it was to share stories and research and technology from medical communities raising awareness for Noonan syndrome around the world. It constantly evolved, and occasionally, it was really exciting.

I could have missed any one of their posts. But after getting that new diagnosis of Harrison's heart, I believe I was meant to find what I did.

A Cardiologist named Dr. Andelfinger in Montreal posted his findings on a new use for a cancer drug called Trametinib in a medical journal, and Noonan Syndrome Hub shared that medical journal.

Dr. Andelfinger had had two three-month-old patients with RAF1 type Noonan syndrome that presented with a Hypertrophic Cardiomyopathy, just like Harrison. Trametinib was used to shrink cancerous cells in tumours, and Dr. Andelfinger had surmised that perhaps it could also be used to shrink cells in extra-thick heart muscles.

After three months on a trial basis, those two babies saw a complete recovery of their hearts.

I swallowed hard. I was not a doctor. I did not know how medicine worked. But I knew deep down that it was extremely important that I pass this medical journal on to our Cardiologist, Dr. Human. So I did.

Not only did he read it, but he responded that Dr. Andelfinger was an old colleague of his, and that he would contact him as soon as possible.

A couple of months went by, and at our next cardiology appointment, Dr. Human told us that he had spoken to Dr. Andelfinger, and they were going to start building a case to bring Trametinib to BC Children's Hospital on a trial basis.

In May of 2019, Harrison had a cardiac MRI to determine if his heart was a candidate for Trametinib. It was.

We had learned to only get excited about something medically involving Harrison when his doctors were excited. And our doctors were ecstatic.

We started making plans to study the side effects with their statistics and sign the paperwork. We felt confident that Harrison was going to become the third child—and only toddler—in the world to try a cancer drug for a heart condition. The potential was groundbreaking.

It was hope the size of a mustard seed, yet big enough to propel us forward.

The Other Shoe (2019)

The hope for Harrison and his upcoming Trametinib treatment made us confident, and we started making more plans for the future. Now that our family had grown by two new members, living with Joe in Abbotsford was no longer sustainable, and we dreamt of having our own place.

Even though her joint pain was to the point that she could no longer walk, I was never able to convince my mom to go see a doctor as she had no more money and no desire to trust Big Pharma. But since she was determined to keep living with us, I persuaded her to apply for an American passport at the US embassy like I had a decade before. Then she could apply for a visitor visa and have some social security money.

We spent a day navigating her wheelchair all over the city, and we were successful in our quest. It took a few months to get sorted out and the money wasn't much, but every little bit helped. Mom would need to reapply for her visitor's visa every eighteen months but she would be here with us, for good. I breathed a sigh of relief. The days of the Butler gals skirting the rules were officially over.

Now that Mom was cleared to live in Canada, Steven and I made plans to move back to Langley, into our own rental house, with room for the kids and my mom too. I had hope that maybe, finally, this would be the last one, the place I could call home.

Moving always meant going through boxes and inevitably digging up memories. Completely by accident, I opened one of my mom's boxes she'd brought down from Hyder, and that's where I found it: Grandmother McCrory's heirloom jewellery Mom had always told me had existed, but I'd never seen except for a few "California pictures." The days when she wore floral print dresses and high heels and makeup, before she tossed them out the window. She was practically a different person now, and she liked it that way.

Obviously, she hadn't tossed everything; I sifted through the ancient jewellery carefully, trying to picture a confident working woman with a morning routine that included these. I thought I recognized a few from those old pictures, and then I came across a small box with two pieces I'd never seen. An absolutely beautiful necklace of a silver flower pendant with two dangling silver feathers, and a silver ring with a large turquoise stone in the middle. Feeling bold, I put the ring on; it only fit my pinky. Maybe Mom had never worn this because it hadn't fit. Where did they come from?

A note tucked into the box had my answer: *For Dorothy. Love, Miles - Christmas 1988.*

The breath left my body. I hadn't seen that name since 2011, although I'd thought about it occasionally. My dad must have given her these the year after I was born. I studied the designs in the silver more closely, and I was almost certain this was authentic Indigenous jewellery. Made in California or perhaps even Mexico.

Maybe the passing of time had given me nostalgic lenses, but I wished I'd stayed in contact with him somehow. I wanted him to see my children. I had so many questions to ask him. The free ancestry website trial I'd done a few months ago had not yielded enough answers for the ache in my heart. All I could do was my own research; most of the (few) books written about my tribe were in Spanish, but I gleaned enough to know in my heart that my ancestors claimed me—that they were hummingbirds watching over me from the afterlife.

But this *knowing* had no bearing on modern-day governmental tribal conditions. I could answer the call to reconnect and learn Hiaki language, I could memorize our stories and honour our history, I could braid my hair and wear beads, I could follow all the Pascua-Yaqui related social media accounts in the world, but they would never caress my face and call me daughter. The one person who might be able to speak on my behalf, my father, could not claim me without exposing his own secrets.

Even though finding the jewellery only brought me pain, I could not bring myself to purge it. I put it back in the thirty-year-old box and tossed it into the closet with the rest of my mom's heirlooms. It could stay in the In Between for now, just like I always had.

This jewellery and the brown eyes of my children would be all I had left of him.

~

On June 26, 2019, our fresh start felt complete when we had our first party at our new house to celebrate the first birthday of Evangeline Rey. There were not one but *two* cakes, unicorn balloons, *Moana* and *Cars* décor. Our tiny queen loved a little bit of everything, and she thrived amongst the twenty or so family and friends who had suddenly filled her space and presented her with shiny new things.

Amidst the delightful chaos, Harrison struggled. He had never cared much for noise, but he seemed particularly sensitive that day. He walked very slowly through people's legs, almost falling a few times. He seemed happiest lying down, watching a cartoon with his bottle, and the party continued on around him.

My empathy would turn to concern and then alarm over the following week. By Canada Day, July 1, Harrison's whole head was extremely puffy and he could barely move. When he tried to walk, he would start shaking and crying, like he was afraid he was going to fall and had no control about how to land. He was barely eating or sleeping, and taking him in the car for longer than five minutes resulted in vomiting.

So, rather than risk an hour-long drive to Children's Hospital, we took him into the Langley emergency room. After we had been there for hours, a family member texted Steve to say, "Make sure you mention mould poisoning. I've noticed Carly and you don't wash his bottles very well because there's always mould in them. That could be what's wrong with him."

My fear and worry started melting down into wrath. But I wouldn't have time to give it room.

Once again, we were surrounded by doctors who hadn't heard of Noonan syndrome and were on the phone with our team at BC Children's.

We were finally admitted with what they said was probably an ear infection. They did bloodwork and started giving him antibiotics. Over the next three days, Harrison continued to get worse. We knew it couldn't be an ear infection.

I made a post on our Noonan Syndrome Facebook page. After many comments of encouragement and advice, I received a private message from a mom in Australia:

"My son (also RAF1) had something very similar happen to him, and he ended up having hydrocephalus (water on the brain) because of a brain tumour. You need to demand that Harrison gets a CT or an MRI of his head right away; I'm only telling you this because my son didn't make it, and every day that passes will make Harrison worse if this is what's going on. All the best."

Fuck. Every once in a while, parents would post about the loss of their child on the Facebook page, and every time, it would sit in my gut like a stone. But I had not seen this woman on the page before. I will be eternally grateful that she opened up the box of her own pain to reach out to me. A stranger in Australia named Dana saved Harrison's life.

I immediately mentioned hydrocephalus to the Langley doctors. They thought it seemed pretty extreme. Steve and I decided that we would give an ultimatum: either get us a transfer via ambulance to BC Children's Hospital, or we would be discharging ourselves and taking him there anyway.

The pediatrician agreed to take a video of Harrison trying to walk so it could be sent to the neurology team at BCCH. Harrison was miserable and he barely lasted being upright long enough for a video to be taken. But it was sent, and the next day, an ambulance transfer was arranged, even though BCCH wasn't sure why we were coming over for an ear infection.

I sat in the front of the rig with the driver, and Steve was in the back with Harrison and another paramedic. For forty-five minutes, the ambulance rocked and bumped and shook, and Harrison screamed in agony. I was covered in sweat, my hands sore from gripping my purse so tightly. I thought we'd never make it.

But we did. We were admitted to the seventh floor, general procedures since they weren't sure what to do with us yet. A social worker had a spare iPad with Harrison's favourite movie *Cars* already downloaded onto it. We ordered him some mac and cheese from the cafeteria, and Denny's delivery for ourselves. For a moment, there was some calm.

The next morning, a Neurology team that had watched the video of Harrison showed up. The head doctor was very brusque and loud; he put Harrison on the floor to watch what he would do. Once again, Harrison started shaking and crying uncontrollably, unable to move. Surely, this wasn't an ear infection, surely it was neurological.

"I don't think it's a neuro thing," the doctor said. "We could order a CT for a week from now, but I'm not sure it's worth sending you guys all over the place when he probably just has an infection."

A week from now? Oh, hell no.

I spoke up. "He's already been like this for over a week, and we live an hour away. We're not going home, we need his head looked at today."

The doctor handled me like an emotional woman, and started filling out orders for Harrison to be seen by all of our doctors for a general checkup. By divine stroke, our first appointment was with Dr. Gardiner, Harrison's eye doctor.

Steve sat in a wheelchair with Harrison on his lap, and we were wheeled down to Ophthalmology. As Dr. Gardiner turned out all the lights and put on her head gear, Harrison didn't even try to fight her looking into his eyes. *Well, now I KNOW something is wrong.* My baby normally hated this kind of contact, and that day, it was like he'd given up.

Dr. Gardiner looked into his eyes for no longer than twenty seconds.

"He's got immense pressure behind both of his eyes, probably hydrocephalus. We need to order an MRI right away."

Yes!

Fuck!

No. God, please, no.

When Harrison was still in the NICU, at two weeks old, he had his first brain MRI, just to "rule that out." He slept like a cherub the entire time, and they were able to get really good pictures of his brain.

I remember looking at the pictures in awe that this kind of technology was even possible. My son's *brain*.

"Everything looks good," the MRI tech said. "He does have one tiny little dark spot behind one of his optic nerves, but that just means he might need glasses someday."

Steve and I looked at each other, our bespectacled selves, and smiled. That we could handle.

On July 5, 2019, at two and a half years old, Harrison had his second brain MRI. Again, he slept peacefully (for the first time in days), but only due to some powerful anesthesia.

We paced around our room, waiting for someone, anyone, to come give us an update. And when we received it, it was from the same exact neurology team we'd been negotiating with from the beginning, minus the head neurologist who had tried to send us home. He'd been replaced by a tall, narrow woman with kind eyes.

She spoke gently. "While Harrison is still sleeping, we'd like to have a meeting with you in the conference room."

Steve and I grabbed each other's hands, holding each other up as we followed these strangers into a room with a long table and cushy black chairs. Air conditioning. A gigantic white board. A pitcher of water and a tissue box.

A planet we'd never been to.

The new head neurologist opened her computer next to us. Once again, I saw pictures of my son's brain, but this time, I was scouring each speck for answers.

She tried to speak in as many laymen's terms as possible: "Harrison has been gradually getting sicker because he has hydrocephalus, fluid building up in his brain. Around six litres of spinal fluid travels back and forth between everyone's brain and spine every single day, but since Harrison's neurological pathways are blocked, his walking has been especially affected, and his head is probably in a lot of pain. See all of these grey pathways here? It should be black, but it's all fluid. Because of these masses right here."

She clicked to a different image, and we gasped as she circled four foreign black tissues all over Harrison's brain, like a vandal had thrown globs of paint onto a priceless work of art. "These gliomas are blocking all the pathways for his spinal fluid, and unfortunately, they are inoperable at this point."

Brain tumours. Just living there like moles, silently accumulating more space with each passing day. One deep in his cerebellum, two near his brain stem, and one right behind his optic nerve.

He might need glasses someday.

I thought of the brain MRI I'd had at Harrison's age, the one that had been so "unique" it turned out to be nothing.

And now an "ear infection" had flipped the script completely.

I could feel myself floating above the room, only tethered by the sweat greasing my husband's hand to mine. I forced myself to form the words, "Where did they come from?" My thoughts were racing.

Maybe I'd given him mould poisoning, after all.

Maybe I looked at my phone while I was feeding him too often, and the magnetic waves infected his brain.

Maybe when I was pregnant, I forgot I had sushi or wine or or or...

"We've learned that sometimes people with genetic disorders like Noonan syndrome can develop a brain tumour, but usually only one. This is extremely uncommon, and we are so sorry to share this news with you. We'll give you a moment, and then we'll reconvene and share our plan of action."

Each team member quietly got up and left the room, one of them pausing to push a tissue box across the table closer to us.

As soon as the door shut, sobs erupted from Steven's body like a wounded animal. I, however, was still floating on the ceiling, expecting to wake up from this nightmare at any moment.

The plan of action was fairly simple: using a tube, they would carve a pathway through Harrison's brain tissue, a way for the fluid to drain on its own, and on the way out, they would take a sample from one of the tumours to test for cancer. We'd have to keep an eye out for the fluid returning, however, as the brain is a miracle muscle that likes to heal itself. A man-made pathway might be vulnerable to self-restoration, and then we'd be right back where we started.

On the morning of Harrison's surgery, I crawled into the giant hospital bed and curled up next to him. He would sleep and then wake in fits and starts, thrashing and wailing, his swollen head finding no comfort. His state had accelerated so fast; I breathed a prayer of thanks that we had brought him in when we did. If we had stayed home, I'd be telling a very different story.

The part of me that had remained numb since hearing the news melted away as I tried to cocoon his tiny body inside of mine. A few close friends came and stood around the bed, speaking prayers and stroking my arm. But I did not see them. I was in a place where no parent should have to go: the possibility of outliving their child. How many moments did we have left? My friends could pray all they wanted, but as far as I was concerned, if God cared, God would prove it. I was the Christ in Gethsemane, asking for this cup to be taken away, without the caveat of conceding my blood, my sweat, my will.

Not my son. Take me instead.

My tears soaked into my baby's matted curls; I could barely whisper into his ear all the things I wanted him to know about his sister, about the world he hadn't seen yet, about how loved he was, just in case this was the last time I ever held him. I said goodbye to him as they wheeled him away; a lifetime of expecting the world to end at any moment had prepared me to keep the earth below my feet. As always, I would swallow and not be swallowed; I would carry on.

I went downstairs for two coffees in a daze, as one does when their two-year-old is having life-altering brain surgery for the first time. As I leaned against the wall waiting for the barista to call my name, I saw a doctor I recognized but couldn't figure out why.

Suddenly, my daze snapped. It was the first head neurologist we'd had when we arrived here, the one who had said Harrison wasn't suffering from a "neuro thing." He was calmly pouring sugar into his coffee without a care; here was my chance to give him one.

"Hey," I said loudly enough to be heard above the barista din.

He looked up and did not register recognition of me. Of course.

"The other day, you told us my son would be fine to wait for a CT, that it wasn't a neuro issue. Well, I thought you'd like to know that he's in the middle of brain surgery right now, you arrogant jackass. Do better next time."

I was shaken out of my daydream with "Order up for Carly!"

The neurologist walked away, his day unruined.

~

Nothing prepared me for seeing my baby come back to the world after surgery. I had been so prepared to lose him that everything I saw and felt and smelled seemed like a dream. Blood and rubber, sweat and pink antiseptic, a nasty incision with a drain tube coming out of his head.

I climbed into bed and wrapped myself around him like I had before he went in, but this time he was much happier. Maybe it was the drugs, maybe it was the fact that his head wasn't swollen with spinal fluid anymore.

They'd successfully carved a path through his brain around the tumours, and the biopsy they'd taken showed that there was no cancer so far. Benign but still invasive. Grateful but still numb.

Two days later, we were cleared to go home. Evie-Rey had stayed with my in-laws so our home looked like a haunting shrine to the people we had been ten days before. Deflated balloons on the floor and rotting birthday cake on the counter felt appropriate.

~

I didn't know how to be a mom who goes grocery shopping and checks her son's head for an infection when she gets home. Who gives antibiotics to one kid and giggly bubble baths to another. Who reads bedtime stories and medical journals about inoperable brain tumours.

We hunkered down at home for the next six weeks. Friends from all over the world said they were praying for us, and one of them created a GoFundMe. We were extremely grateful for that, because even though so many aspects of healthcare were covered in Canada, we still had to pay for food and parking and any necessities.

Finally, it seemed like we were in the clear for healing physically, and with bills piling up, Steve went back to work even though it took all his strength to get out the door. Two days later, Harrison started vomiting and wouldn't get off the floor, his head incision bubbling with angry fluid.

His brain had done what it was supposed to do and healed itself. The man-made tunnel was gone, and Harrison would need another round of surgery to implant a programmable shunt behind his right ear. It would be placed on the lowest setting to keep spinal fluid constantly flowing. We would need to keep a constant eye, as a shunt is still a foreign object in the body and could be rejected with infection at literally any time.

I spent my thirty-second birthday in hospital with my husband and son, once again separated from my tiny daughter.

I had thought it was safe to plan a birthday gathering a few weeks earlier, but I cancelled it. People sent more money and more prayers.

On October 7, I treated myself to a free coffee and a walk to the nearby Safeway to buy myself a Betty Crocker Microwave Mug Cake. It would take all my energy to put the packet of powder in the mug, add water, and nuke it for two minutes; it might as well be delicious.

But that night, Harrison went to sleep, and Steve said something very uncharacteristic of him: "Want to go for a walk?"

I did, but I glanced at our sleeping boy. "Can we leave?"

"I've already asked the nurse to keep an eye on him. Come on." He seemed in a hurry, and while I was completely exhausted, I felt a small smile creeping through. We were in this life for the long haul; we had to still try and be The Buttons.

Each floor at BC Children's Teck Acute building has a Family Room with a small kitchen, table and couches. At this time of night, ours should have been quiet, but I saw decorations and presents, and nonchalantly said, "Oh, someone is having a party. That's nice."

To my confusion, Steve started to walk into that Family Room and pulled my hand to join him. "Love, we can't go in there, it's—"

And then all of a sudden, five of my friends burst out of the Lactation Room next door, yelling "Surprise!" and singing "Happy Birthday."

I immediately broke down crying. I had always wanted a surprise birthday party, but it wasn't really Steve's forte, and that was fine.

But he had been collaborating with all of these dear people—including getting a video message from Sirius in America to share—for a while, and I'd had no idea. We spent two hours completely forgetting that we were in a Children's Hospital; it was laughter and sugar and delight. Finally, an understanding of joy in the midst of Apocalypse not because we were in denial but because it was necessary. An oasis in the desert. I fell in love all over again.

~

Ever since I'd discovered the use of Trametinib in early 2019 on children with RAF1 type Noonan syndrome for their heart conditions, we'd pushed for Harrison to be approved as the third kid worldwide. Again, I was obviously not a doctor, but I wondered if it was possible to kill two birds with one stone, as Trametinib was already a drug whose job was to shrink tumour cells. Harrison's were benign, but wouldn't the medicine still know what to do?

Right after Harrison's fourth brain surgery in October 2019, our cardiologist Dr. Human and our oncologist Dr. Hukin started collaborating. They were extremely intrigued and excited at the possibility of being able to shrink the cells that thickened Harrison's heart muscle and shrink the cells that grew his tumours at the same time. They commended me for bringing it up.

The next hurdle was financial. We were approved for Trametinib to be brought to BC Children's Hospital, but it would cost us $2,400 a month to give him one pill a day. The exact cost of our rent. Since his heart condition prevented him from trying any other form of chemotherapy, and since he didn't have cancer to begin with, we had to beg BC Cancer to have mercy on us. We were ready to give up our house if necessary, but in the end, they said yes.

We began to prepare for our son to be the first kid ever to try Trametinib for a heart condition *and* brain tumours in the year 2020.

We had no way of knowing that the world as we knew it was about to end, for everyone.

All we had in those last few weeks of 2019 was knowing that my mom was safe, Harrison's shaved curls were starting to grow back, Evie-Rey was learning how to scream-sing "Thunderstruck" by AC/DC, and our home was warm with the company of friends.

~

I started sharing more of our medical journey on public social media. After all, this was how we'd connected with other Noonan syndrome parents in the first place, to the point of saving Harrison's life. Maybe someone else out there had just gotten a diagnosis too, and our family could help them through it.

I was often asked by strangers what the hardest thing is about being a medical disability parent. Years ago, I would have said it was the NICU, but I was naïve. It took me a while to really land on an answer. In reality, the hardest thing was the fact that I didn't know how long this was going to last. I might be responsible for my child's every need until the end of time, or I might get only one more day. Both of those possibilities scared me to death. The uncertainty reminds me, for good or ill, of living in that cabin in the woods with my mom for all those years, waiting for the world to end. It might end any day now—or not at all.

I took comfort in the truth that it would be different for Harrison and Evie. He was three and she was seventeen months, and they were not about to learn of Heaven and Hell, of sin and saving. They were good as they were, and they'd been through enough already. I had to believe that I had broken the cycle of fatherless children and angry Creators and having no roots to call home. Healing was their birthright now.

My world had ended many times since I first knew it could. I knew now that my mom only did what scared mothers have done for thousands of years; I knew now that if you really believe something, you will act on it no matter the price. I still didn't know why I survived while so many others did not.

Apocalypse had tried to chase me down and swallow me whole for years—but I was still here.